The Solution-Focused Educator

The Solution-Focused Educator

*Breakthrough Strategies for Teachers and
School Administrators to
Reframe Their Mindsets*

Todd Elliott Franklin

ROWMAN & LITTLEFIELD
Lanham • Boulder • New York • London

Published by Rowman & Littlefield
An imprint of The Rowman & Littlefield Publishing Group, Inc.
4501 Forbes Boulevard, Suite 200, Lanham, Maryland 20706
www.rowman.com

Unit A, Whitacre Mews, 26-34 Stannary Street, London SE11 4AB

British Library Cataloguing in Publication Information Available

Library of Congress Cataloging-in-Publication Data Available

ISBN 9781475837797 (hardback : alk. paper) | ISBN 9781475837803 (pbk. : alk. paper) | ISBN
9781475837810 (electronic)

∞ ™ The paper used in this publication meets the minimum requirements of American
National Standard for Information Sciences Permanence of Paper for Printed Library
Materials, ANSI/NISO Z39.48-1992.

Printed in the United States of America

Contents

Foreword

When Todd Elliott Franklin, a Fairfax County Public School principal, first pitched me the idea for his book, I was both intrigued and fascinated by the concepts he put forward about the term *mindset* in a school setting. After presenting at a conference at the Wintergreen Resort in Roseland, Virginia, Todd approached me about writing a foreword to his book, *The Solution-Focused Educator*. We walked together for about fifteen minutes and Todd spoke to me about what his goals were with the writing and how he felt it offered needed solutions for the mindset of today's educators. I asked him to keep in touch with me and offered my support as he moved forward. Once he signed his book contract with Rowman & Littlefield, we spoke again, and I was happy to write the foreword to his book.

A very unique feature to the writing, at the beginning, is the self-assessment. This awareness tool helps teachers and administrators better understand their current mindset in the school. As Todd states, "It will help you see how you relate to yourself *first* before you relate to the students and teachers (and before you read the book)."

Through our discussions, it was clear to me that the focus of his book was unique. It is one of the very few books on the market that centers on cognitive reframing/mindset strategies *for a specific professional niche*—educators only (teachers and administrators).

Though the goal of the book is centered on refocusing a task-driven mind in the classroom and the school, the writing aims to establish a deeper understanding about the relationship between problem identification and the anxiety that ensues. Through various school-based vignettes, Todd looks at the habits of the mind that initially create negative emotional reactions for teachers and administrators. He then provides solutions for those mood-altering reactions that can move teachers and administrators from a feeling of frustration to emotional contentment, simply by anticipating and reframing throughout the day.

Because the complexity of demands on classroom teachers and administrators is becoming more and more intense each year, it is important for educators to understand how to control the only thing they can: their mindset. Because this is not something that is taught extensively in graduate programs and the professional development around this concept is minimal, Todd's writing invites educators to reinvent their approach to the job itself.

Unlike many other motivational books for teachers and administrators, Todd captures the metacognition aspect for educators by taking the predictable thought processes around daily concerns and reframing them for the better. His storytelling and solutions around how to process problems internally and reframe negative thought habits allow Todd to meet the mindset needs of the novice teacher, the seasoned instructor, and the school-based administrator.

Through his usage of the symbol of a triangle, Todd consistently makes the mindset concepts easy to understand. He utilizes this shape as a strong representational pattern that clearly illustrates how educators can mentally diagram problematic issues, outline their emotional reactions to them, and create a new attitude of solvability. With practice, these reframing strategies become habitual. After reading this book, school-based personnel will better understand the causes of their stress and accept their reactions—but will be better equipped to move forward without attitudinal impact.

Successful educators have an ability to master their emotions. They do this in a way that does not inhibit their ability to teach the students, govern the school, or understand the unique needs of parents and colleagues. If one is in the educational business long enough, he or she encounters individuals in a curriculum team meeting, a faculty meeting, or in the lounge who cannot find the positive energy bus. They are stuck with their own opinions, struggle to see new ideas, and have a propensity to intoxicate the culture of the staff.

In *The Solution-Focused Educator*, teachers and administrators will learn *how not to get bogged down* by these individuals. Instead of, consciously or subconsciously, needing them to change to feel better, Todd is able to show educators *how to migrate their own way around these people to a better experience*. Through his insightful mindset strategies and support mechanisms, Todd is able to give educators the tools they need for working with typical school-based issues and moving toward a more positive pathway to job satisfaction.

Drawing on a variety of teacher observations, professional development symposiums, and information disseminated via principals and division-wide superintendents, in his book, Todd examines the causal effects of stress and its impact on the ability of teachers and administrators to effectively problem solve in a school setting.

Teachers and administrators are consistently juggling the ever-changing expectations placed upon their craft. By discussing e-mail/social networking challenges, contentious parent conferences, and colleague disputes, among many other issues, Todd brings the reader through step-by-step instructions for attitudinal change, providing alternative solutions to those annual concerns that educators face.

The true value in his book lies in the real-world connections Todd is able to make with authentic scenarios from the classrooms to the main office. Throughout the book, Todd shows how teachers and administrators can dissect their habitual tendencies for the better. Whether you are a teacher, a school-based administrator, or a specialist, Todd's book serves as an excellent *"summer read" or "beginning of the year kickoff"* for educators who want to think differently.

The reason I believe in and endorse the writing in this book is simple: Todd has provided the educators of today with a fresh outlook for how to better control their mindset toward the classroom, students, parents, and colleagues. By offering a different prism to interpret problems and reframing mindsets for the better, *The Solution-Focused Educator* serves as a valuable resource for not just changing the culture of the school, but changing the mindset of the individual teacher and administrator attached to the school building.

I am excited for Todd's book as he outlines a unique and progressive approach for how teachers and administrators can develop a new classroom mindset and close, what he refers to as, their personal achievement gap.

Todd Whitaker
Professor of Educational Leadership, University of Missouri
Professor Emeritus, Indiana State University
Author of national best seller *What Great Teachers Do Differently*

Preface

The Solution-Focused Educator is a roadmap for educators to create a mentality that is best equipped to tackle new challenges and initiatives in a school setting. The goal is for teachers and school leaders to better understand how to reshape preconditioned responses to annual stressors. The premise is centered on modeling an emotional regimen that is focused on personal development and improvement.

The writing is based on more than twenty years of research, personal anecdotal records, observations, and conversations from people who have served in the classroom for many years, led school buildings and school districts, and, simultaneously, raised their own families. Though the focus is centered on refocusing a task-driven mind in the classroom, the book aims to establish a deeper understanding about the intimate relationship between problem identification and the anxiety that ensues within this psychological dyad.

I wrote about this process in the context of a school setting. However, the mentality competency and its framework are applicable to a variety of office cultures and family dynamics. From the hallways to the classrooms, teachers and administrators remain deeply enmeshed in the ever-changing expectations placed upon their craft. Drawing on a variety of observations of teachers, administrators, professional development symposiums, and multiple division superintendents, I examined the causal effects of stress and its impact on the ability to effectively problem solve in a school setting.

I discovered some similarities for how many teachers and administrators define these prisms. By documenting and analyzing these embedded habits and aligning them with an individual's aspirations to change, I discovered how educators could problem solve more effectively by reframing their mental approach.

The solutions offered in the book establish a new toolbox for personnel working in the schools. In his book *Emotional Intelligence*, Daniel Goleman discusses the importance of learning how to bring intelligence to emotion. With the growing responsibilities placed upon educators, how does one learn to *bring intelligence to emotion*? In a survey of parents and teachers, Goleman discusses a growing trend for the present generation of children whereby they seem to be experiencing more feelings of loneliness, depression, and impulsivity. He speaks to the remedy as being focused on how we prepare students for life in reference to educating them on the platform of emotional intelligence. He mentions learning blocks based on self-control, self-awareness, and empathy (Goleman 1995). I believe this to be true.

In order for the individual teacher, in all of us, to better understand emotional intelligence, there needs to be a deeper reflection for how we view the mirror. Are the growing trends of loneliness, depression, and impulsivity that Goleman describes simply related to the present generation of children, or could those attributes be applied to educators in the workplace as well?

This book will provide those needed reflections in order for the individual reader to dissect those habitual tendencies to move forward with change. It is incumbent upon teachers and administrators to further understand how to navigate the relationship between emotional intelligence and the mindset that is brought to the school and the classroom. By making this a mental habit, you can become a leader for your *mindset* and perhaps react differently to the experiences that seemingly always breed stress, anxiety, or confusion.

By transforming the relationship you have with stress, you can develop a new classroom mindset and close what I refer to as your personal achievement gap. In order to best understand the construct around this concept, I embedded a framework of personal development triangles within the writing. The initial diagram, seen in figure P.1, displays the construct itself in regard to how stimulants (stress) are linked to emotions.

I titled these triangular shapes: Hurricane-GIANTS. Every day, you experience a *hurricane of thoughts and feelings* in reaction to specific events. Learning how to *Get Involved and Not Take Sides* (GIANTS) with one emotion too much, where your mood is impacted, is a constant struggle. The triangle concept represents the challenge and the solution: How do you *get involved* with the experiences that are shaping your mood for the day *and not take sides* with one high or low emotion? The shape is simply an analogy that creates a visual, which in turn encourages individuals to categorize their experiences. For many individuals, their emotional reactions are quite concretized—embedded into the habits of the mind.

Mindset strategies should not be lost or confused with the term *mindfulness*. Though an advocate for some of this work, I believe the term *mindfulness* can be, at times, too ambiguous for many people. The concept sounds good, but maintaining the momentum to practice it becomes the problem. It

THE PERSONAL DEVELOPMENT TRIANGLE

BROKEN WHITE LINE:

THIS REPRESENTS THE ONLY LINE OF THE TRIANGLE THAT CAN BE REFRAMED.

MAKE A HABIT OUT OF BECOMING MORE METACOGNITIVE.

YOUR ATTITUDE CAN THEN BECOME THE NEGOTIABLE ENTITY, IN THE TRIANGLE, THAT *YOU CAN CONTROL.*

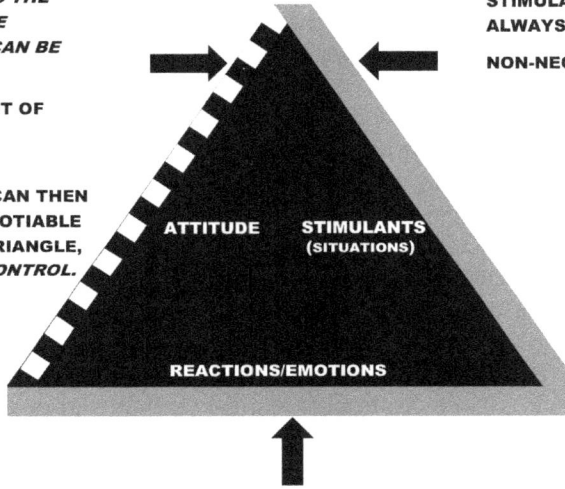

SOLID GRAY LINE #1:

STIMULANTS WILL ALWAYS EXIST.

NON-NEGOTIABLE

ATTITUDE   STIMULANTS
(SITUATIONS)

REACTIONS/EMOTIONS

SOLID GRAY LINE #2:

YOUR REACTIONS OR EMOTIONS ABOUT THE STIMULANTS WILL ALWAYS EXIST.

STIMULANTS ARE MARRIED TO EMOTIONS.

NON-NEGOTIABLE

Figure P.1. The Personal Development Triangle. Graphic by Todd Franklin

is helpful when you learn something new for it to be tangible, something you can grab onto and apply. The most successful, sustained learning strategies are the ones that teach you *signposts* to help you break away from your normal thought patterns.

Breaking through the concretized belief systems of your past is quite a challenge. How do leaders of schools create shift changes? How do teachers recognize and develop an authentic reasoning with themselves to change? Constant and continuous learning cycles of professional development are not always the answer. As seen in this "Formulas for Success" diagram, personal development should trump professional development in order to possess a mindset that is truly ready to change. In fact, the personal construct of the individual educator needs to be shifted in order for professional development to be effective and authentic.

OBSERVATIONS WERE THE KEY

I have observed many classroom teachers who crave mind-disciplined approaches that would help them gain a healthier perspective on challenging work-related issues. For more than twenty years, I observed individuals with various educational, cultural, and familial backgrounds. I documented how they perceived problems during their school day and what contributed to their anxiety. I needed to learn how effective leaders of organizations (both in the classroom, in the school, and in central offices) transitioned people away from a victim's mentality.

I needed to know how the positive, effective teachers and administrators established a leadership role over misguided thoughts; where blaming outside entities for perceived problems was no longer a habit of the mind. By learning these keys, I saw firsthand how successful leaders create a culture for themselves and their subordinates that makes people thirsty to try something different. The novice teacher and the veteran warrior of the classroom can learn to reframe their mindset for the better.

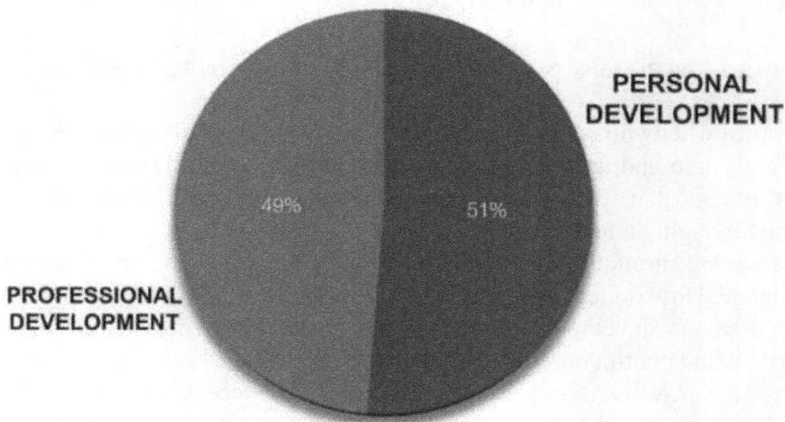

Figure P.2. Formulas for Success. Graphic produced using Keynote template by Todd Franklin

This book aims to support school personnel on how to better recognize everyday challenges and rise above the fray that is not always centered on teaching and learning. Some of the solutions are quite simple and straightforward, while others beg for the reader to dig deeper for conceptual understanding.

I wrote about scenarios that would offer solutions to long-standing challenges. The real-world examples allow you to see how to shift your problem solving away from needing others to change first. Through these vignettes, I attempted to bridge the emotional divide that exists between *problem solving with a compressed mentality* and *adhering to the systematic initiatives that create the perceived stress.*

As you work with children every day, your own mind can become staggered and chaotic. It is far too easy to lose perspective on what should matter most. Though you need to be more centered on your own family, friends, and so on, you may struggle to find those methods that will support your desires to have that unencumbered mental space. Much of your emotional energy (even while driving home) may be spent living in the lanes and lives of students, parents, administrators, and colleagues. As an educator, because your focus is on others for the majority of your day, your mind can become compressed. You may begin to lose sight of that openness and flexibility that you once prided yourself on throughout any given school year.

In one of my favorite books, *Feeling Great: The Educator's Guide for Eating Better, Exercising Smarter and Feeling Your Best*, Todd Whitaker and James Winkle speak to taking care of ourselves first, so we can better take care of others. Their book speaks to the obvious health benefits exercise can have on the state of mind for a classroom teacher. Much of my focus in this book is aimed at reshaping one's attitude toward perceived obstacles; one of which is the lack of time.

Whitaker and Winkle point out, "Though we all feel that we do not have enough extra time to focus on taking care of ourselves, we do somehow find the time to gripe, whine, or complain about not having the time! We really do have enough time to do what is most important, we just have to decide that taking care of ourselves needs to be higher up on that list. It is amazing, but somehow, we make ourselves feel that so many things in life are urgent. However, effective people, somehow or another, even with all of the things that seem urgent, still make sure that they have time for what is important" (Whitaker and Winkle 2002).

Tackling the task of making time for physical exercise, just like tackling the task of teaching students or managing a building, cannot start without learning how to conquer a compressed mindset. How do specific teachers and leaders seem to possess those uncanny healthy perspectives on life? They seem to turn the stuck cycle around before September. As compared to some of their colleagues, they don't seem to possess the same thoughts, emotions, and reactions to certain situations. They have that healthy "it" factor that makes them different in a good kind of way.

How do they do it? What makes them possess that "high on life" attitude? Through this project, I discovered similarities in how educators tend to focus their approach to problem solving. I charted the typical stressors and how many of us normally reacted to them. The following three specific mental stances were found to be most common stimulants to stress:

- This ("some decision or directive") is unfair to me.
- My time ("I could be getting something else done") is being impacted.
- I worry about what others think of my disposition or decision making (parents, administration, superintendent, etc.).

For many years, your mental dialogue may travel these three roads and arrive at destination points titled Stressed and Confused. Please note that each of these interpretations contains a "me" or "my" statement. These egocentric compressed positions are normal, but these thoughts are the cause to becoming stuck. You may find yourself challenged to produce the lifestyle you want to lead.

Our life in the school often revolves around the *whens* of the calendar:

- When are grades due?
- When is the next team meeting or department in-service?
- When are late bus schedules or when are "specials"?
- When are we testing?
- When are the parent conferences?
- When are the teacher workdays?

THE SELF-ASSESSMENT

I always view the beginning of a school year like New Year's Eve: it is time to make resolutions and start fresh. Much of the material focuses on our preconditioned response mechanisms. In other words, how does your conditioning for so many years drive your decision making? How do you typically react? What does your usual mental dialogue sound like? These are the questions that may be most helpful to ask yourself throughout the book.

The names, stories, places, and scenarios have all been altered in order to protect the confidentiality of the personnel I have worked with over the years. Thus, in the end, the book serves as a simple roadmap for how to reshape the established culture of an educator's mind for the better. Essentially, in any given September, you can create a development plan for yourself with a strict focus on self-inquiry and analysis.

The very first portion of the book is devoted to a self-assessment. The Me-Self Assessment (ME-SA) is simply an awareness tool to help you better understand your current mindset and how you may approach your job. It will help you see how you relate to yourself first before you relate to students, colleagues, and parents. The ME-SA challenges the current culture of your mind by asking you to assess the quality of your relationship with yourself.

The results will provide you with a reflection for how you *may approach* the day, students, and other job responsibilities. The goal for you is to discover some critical insights as to how you can better become a leader of your mind as opposed to a reactor to its experiences. The assessment coupled with this book should help teach you how to best serve yourself in this complex triangular relationship of teaching, learning, and self-actualization.

For the assessment, it is important that you answer all of the questions from the standpoint of how you *currently relate to the challenges of the school day*—your current mindset. For teachers, some of the questions may indirectly ask you to think along an administrator's continuum. For administrators, some of the questions may indirectly ask for you to hark back to your teaching days in the classroom.

For the best results, you need to focus on the statements and choose the best descriptor that matches your interpretations or internal dialogue most consistently. As you read the items, you want to choose the one that makes you say, "Yes, I think like that a lot!" *You want to avoid choosing the one that looks better or the one that you may feel like you need to mark.* Once you gain a more authentic understanding of how you think along a specific continuum and you process the "why" behind your choices, you will better understand how to reframe your mindset for the school year. You will begin to recognize how to resolve problematic situations externally before they define your emotional state internally.

Finally, there is no score for this assessment. The process itself is the feedback. The assessment contains an obvious pattern. The pattern that you sense is the basis for all of the learning. It will quickly become obvious to you how this professional development exercise is structured. Some of the statements in the assessment ask for you to choose how you might typically think and feel. Some are just a few words. It is up to you to choose the one that best symbolizes how you typically think, feel, and interpret events and emotions in your life. Because the content is solely based on my personal observations and anecdotal evidence, the assessment itself and the following descriptions are far from any type of formalized indicator spawned from a longitudinal study.

Thus, at the end of the assessment, there are two very brief constructs that should only be viewed as guidelines for understanding some of your habitual attitudes toward the classroom/school, the job, and your temperament. It is important to note that the descriptions within these two categories should not be concretized as one or the other. It is human nature to possess both. These categorical descriptions are simply an attempt to bring further details to your results.

I would strongly suggest that you take the assessment before you begin any of the reading. The book will provide you with a new toolbox that will extend that euphoric emotion you feel at the beginning of summer and, hopefully, make it an ongoing, yearlong experience.

Acknowledgments

I would first like to thank my wife, Maureen, and my three young children, Brendan, Julia, and Ryan, who have provided me the love and support and encouragement to see this project through its completion. Your humor and enthusiasm served as a catalyst for me to continue to work through some of the most difficult writing blocks but, most importantly, through many challenging life experiences. I love you and I am grateful for your unwavering encouragement and abundance of love over many, many years.

I am grateful for my mother and father, Elisabeth and John Franklin, who provided me an education and an open platform to pursue my passion around writing and working to provide support for others. The countless failed writing attempts in high school, where my mother would proofread and mark up my papers, served as motivation to constantly try to get it right the next time and the next time.

I would like to thank the Fairfax County Public School system, which has provided me an education since second grade and continues to employ me to this day. A very special gratitude goes out to all of my teachers and role models, who have served as my mentors and led me down the right path in so many different ways. To that end, I would also like to thank my professors at George Mason University, who, without knowing it at the time, truly played a large role in developing my ability to put words to paper in a coherent fashion. Failing English 101 was a wake-up call, but it was one of the best learning lessons I ever received.

In addition to the above mentioned, this book never would have come to fruition without having such wonderful friends, colleagues, and supervisors who helped guide me, redirect me, and ultimately served as a great support over the years. Your influences and the experiences we continue to share serve as my constant teacher every day. The staffs I have worked with over the years are true leaders for students. I am very thankful for your unwavering companionship, our relationships, and, most of all, the laughs we continue to share.

Finally, I would like to thank the personnel at Rowman & Littlefield who believed in me and my writing. You gave me the opportunity and the platform to pursue an idea, a belief, and a passion around how to help classroom teachers and school administrators.

Once again, I want to express much love and gratitude to everyone who helped guide and support me over the years. This project has been a joy to put together.

Understanding Your Current Mindset before Generating Solutions

The ME-SA

The Me-Self Assessment

1.
A) _____ Life is too busy. I have to go.
B) _____ Life is busy—but whatever—it will all work out.

2.
A) _____ There is not enough time in the day. I must do this now.
B) _____ It will get done whenever.

3.
A) _____ I review my day verbally and mentally all the way home.
B) _____ I do not bring my work home (mental gossip is controlled).

4.
A) _____ I know I am right often. I believe it.
B) _____ Don't care if I am right or wrong—whatever works.

5.
A) _____ I rarely laugh. Crisis management is a staple. I need to stay ahead.
B) _____ I find myself trying to laugh often during the week.

6.
A) _____ Very anxious as the day begins
B) _____ Slow entry

7.
A) _____ Socializing and befriending colleagues is OK—not needed.
B) _____ Befriending others is very important to me on the job.

8.
A) _____ I often seem to have personality conflicts at work.
B) _____ I am content and quiet and don't make a lot of noise.

9.
A) _____ I blame often.
B) _____ I do not.

10.
A) _____ Because of my life experiences, I am very different nowadays.
B) _____ I am who I am—always have been.

11.
A) _____ This is so wrong. This is not right. This needs to be fixed.
B) _____ It may be wrong but in the big scheme of things—whatever.

12.
A) _____ Confrontation is part of life. I'm ready and welcome it.
B) _____ Confrontation is something I try to avoid.

13.
A) _____ I communicate in e-mail—quickest.
B) _____ I always call.

14.
A) _____ Philosophy: The interim is the wake-up call to parents.
B) _____ Philosophy: I call ahead of time. Timely communication is key.

15.
A) _____ I write paragraphs explaining misbehaviors about students.
B) _____ If I write anything at all, it is two to three sentences max.

16.
A) _____ I become frustrated with people who disagree with me.
B) _____ Agree/disagree . . . does it really matter?

17.
A) _____ I compare my life to others often.
B) _____ I really do not think of others in comparison to myself.

18.
A) _____ Show me the data or I am not changing my ways.
B) _____ If you want me to change what I do—just tell me.

19.
A) _____ Self-help—better-yourself philosophies—hogwash.
B) _____ I believe in the self-help category.

20.
A) _____ I have some bad habits but it is what it is—I need to move on.
B) _____ I have some bad habits; I would like to improve.

21.
A) _____ I find myself wanting things to change quite often.
B) _____ I like the status quo—it is what it is.

22.
A) _____ Work is racing through my mind—I e-mail at night.
B) _____ I leave work at work—not responding to e-mail at night.

23.
A) _____ Data drives everything I do.
B) _____ Data is important, but I am not wedded to having it all the time.

24.
A) _____ Opinions are surface—other people's thoughts—whatever.
B) _____ The opinions of others matter to me a lot.

25.
A) _____ I need to be challenged or I get bored.
B) _____ I accept what is.

26.
A) _____ I rarely doubt myself. I know what works.
B) _____ I am in a constant state of doubting myself—lack confidence.

27.
A) _____ Part of leadership = confront those individuals toxic to the staff.
B) _____ Part of leadership = find work-arounds without direct confrontation.

28.
A) _____ I need to escalate concerns to management often—somebody does.
B) _____ Let somebody else carry the torch to management.

29.
A) _____ I know I lack a balance in life—but don't most of us?
B) _____ I may lack a balance at times—always open to making it better.

30.
A) _____ I need structure, predictability in order to accomplish my goals.
B) _____ Figure it out as we go.

31.
A) _____ I need to know how the administration is disciplining.
B) _____ Once I send a student down to the office, it is their decision.

32.
A) _____ Observe me—no problem—anytime.
B) _____ Observe me—ok—now I feel stressed—I need to plan.

33.
A) _____ Kids need more accountability, experience consequences.
B) _____ Kids are kids. I'm not worried about lack of consequences.

34.
A) _____ I take care of 99 percent of my problems on the phone.
B) _____ I dwell on responses. It takes hours to compose an e-mail.

35.
A) _____ Think more like: "My parents never would have allowed that."
B) _____ Think more like: "I am not going to jump into another's lane"?

36.
A) _____ When people underperform, I take it personally.
B) _____ When people underperform, I don't take it personally.

37.
A) _____ Are they ever going to fix this copier? It is so frustrating!
B) _____ Are they ever going to fix this copier? Oh well, I'll just figure it out.

38.
A) _____ Process is important for a short time. Then, move on.
B) _____ Process and discussion are important. I need to talk things out.

39.
A) _____ Being a teacher is my role. It is not who I am.
B) _____ Being a teacher is who I am. It defines me.

40.
A) _____ I often need to make decisions quickly and move forward.
B) _____ I often need to think for a long time before making a decision.

41.
A) _____ I post it all online. Students need to check it themselves.
B) _____ Students *should* write down their tasks assigned, but I enable.

42.
A) _____ I am the one who sets the tone for the classroom.
B) _____ Often, students will create the rules for the classroom.

43.
A) _____ I believe my job is to teach students.
B) _____ I believe my job is to teach people but teach life skills as well.

44.
A) _____ I like to have a say in exactly what is going to happen each year.
B) _____ I let others provide direction. I am more of a hands-off manager.

45.
A) _____ I focus on what others should be doing or should have done.
B) _____ I focus on what others want me to do—then I just do it.

46. (Initial Internal Reactions)
A) _____ Another mandate from Human Resources—I'm overwhelmed.
B) _____ Another mandate from Human Resources—let's just get it done.

47.
A) _____ I can't believe they are making us do this. This is so frustrating.
B) _____ I don't find myself saying, "I can't believe . . ."

48.
A) _____ This is not fair. I don't like this. This needs to change.
B) _____ I accept and move on.

49.
A) _____ I rush out of bed; I rush to get coffee; I rush to work.
B) _____ Life is not an emergency.

50.
A) _____ Final grades are what the student earned—those are final.
B) _____ After consultation and further review, grades can fluctuate.

51.
A) _____ Student results drive how successful I feel.
B) _____ Results are symbols of performance—not a direct reflection on me.

52.
A) _____ I rarely question my mental constructs. I know who I am.
B) _____ Mental constructs should forever be evaluated.

53.
A) _____ Over the years, I become more frustrated with the profession.
B) _____ Over the years, I find myself very satisfied with this job.

54.
A) _____ I am not patient.
B) _____ I am patient.

55.
A) _____ I state my opinion. It means something.
B) _____ My opinion is a pixel in the larger scheme.

56.
A) _____ Compliments are nice, but I don't need them.
B) _____ Compliments are nice, and I like to hear them often.

57.
A) _____ I am climbing the ladder—there is no turning back.
B) _____ I am climbing the ladder, but I could very easily go back later.

58.
A) _____ Too much involvement from the outside—trust us more.
B) _____ I like the high level of involvement from the outside.

59.
A) _____ I don't mind if people criticize me—better be able to back it up.
B) _____ I am bothered by criticism. It really puts me in a funk.

60.
A) _____ Solutions first
B) _____ Process first

61.
A) _____ To be quite honest, I do not get much out of the meetings I attend.
B) _____ Oftentimes, I find meetings to be informative and worth my time.

62.
A) _____ I am who I am. I am complex—you get what you get.
B) _____ I am who I am, but hopefully that can change—I would like that.

63.
A) _____ My internal dialogue tends to judge persons, places, and things.
B) _____ My internal dialogue often stays positive without judging.

64.
A) _____ I am the adult. I am the authority figure. People need to know that.
B) _____ I am the adult, but I do not *need* to be *the* authority figure.

65.
A) _____ Have not considered backward design as a life method for planning.
B) _____ Backward design is how I start my day—what and how.

66.
A) _____ "Ugh, when do I have to go back to work in August?"
B) _____ Each school year brings new challenges. "I'm ready."

67.
A) _____ I find it difficult not to categorize behaviors, draw conclusions.
B) _____ Projecting = I am focusing on the wrong thing—being unfair.

68.
A) _____ I lecture a lot. My philosophy is top-down. Must know this stuff.
B) _____ Rarely is the classroom teacher driven—very free flowing.

69.
A) _____ Sunday afternoon blues = 4:45 pm, got to go back to the grind.
B) _____ Sunday afternoon is unencumbered by thoughts about work.

70.
A) _____ I'm about academic results in my classroom, bottom line.
B) _____ There is no bottom line. I'm not linear, everything matters.

71.
A) ____ It is very important.
B) ____ Life is too short for anything to be very important.

72.
A) ____ I don't care if I am not invited to the social event.
B) ____ Not being considered for social events would bother me.

73.
A) ____ I juggle a thousand things. It is difficult, but must keep it going.
B) ____ I juggle a thousand things, drop some balls, but whatever.

74.
A) ____ Each person is different, yet a lot seems the same, names change.
B) ____ You never know what is going on in each person's life.

75.
A) ____ I am a "means to an end" person.
B) ____ I am not driven by absolutes.

76.
A) ____ My boss would say: good educator but has some challenges.
B) ____ My boss would say: good educator all around, no reservations.

77.
A) ____ My plate is full.
B) ____ My plate is not that full.

78.
A) ____ Stress is common in my life. I lose sleep.
B) ____ Stress is expected. I don't lose sleep.

79.
A) ____ I find self-reflection time consuming—never worked for me.
B) ____ Self-reflection is a staple for me.

80.
A) ____ I exercise.
B) ____ I don't exercise.

81.
A) ____ I add story lines often to my problems. My mind just races 24/7.
B) ____ Experiences are pixels. They are one of millions—so be them.

82.
A) _____ I don't fixate on the past and dwell about how things use to be.
B) _____ I find myself living in nostalgia often—oh, how things use to be.

83.
A) _____ Self-assessment tools are interesting, doesn't change me.
B) _____ Self-assessment tools are important, and I take time for them often.

84. As each school day begins, influencing myself starts with recognizing who that self is—teacher, principal, parent, spouse. Perhaps I should start with recognizing that those are simply roles I play each day—not my true self.
A) _____ I don't understand. Mostly gobbledygook to me.
B) _____ I understand. The moment I read this passage, I got it.

85.
A) _____ Life is difficult. It is taxing in so many ways.
B) _____ Life is good.

86.
A) _____ Good/Bad, Right/Wrong
B) _____ There is always another way to view a problem.

87. The act of repression transitions to resentment, which causes reflection. Over the years, wisdom is born because of these emotional acts. Is this true?
A) _____ Disagree (mostly because this is gobbledygook to me)
B) _____ Agree (never thought of it this way but could be true)

88.
A) _____ If I'm constantly judged by others, it does not bother me.
B) _____ I often feel like I am being judged by somebody. It bothers me.

89.
A) _____ I need to be heard when I have something to say.
B) _____ I don't need to share my opinion.

90.
A) _____ I am struggling to discover some of the joy I once had at work.
B) _____ I am still embracing many rewarding experiences at work.

91.
A) _____ This is how I feel. This happened, and I need to tell you.
B) _____ I avoid telling a story about my challenges to people.

92.
A) _____ Who I am at home is not that much different from school.
B) _____ Who I am at home is a whole lot different from the classroom.

93.
A) _____ I keep rules up every year. They are etched in stone.
B) _____ I discuss the meaning of my rules all year. They change.

94.
A) _____ In August, I have to plan for the whole year on my calendar.
B) _____ I will learn my schedule as we go.

95.
A) _____ My classroom/office has been structured the same way for years.
B) _____ I change for constructive reasons—need something different.

96. Which do you have in your classroom/office most often?
A) _____ Motivational statements about improving attitude and character
B) _____ Pictures of people, family, friends

97.
A) _____ It seems like one thing after another. It consumes me.
B) _____ A busy schedule is expected, doesn't consume me.

98.
A) _____ Mental muscle? Never thought about exercising it.
B) _____ The mental muscle is a term I am familiar with.

99.
A) _____ I do not practice with the small stuff.
B) _____ I recognize the trivial. I do not engage.

100.
A) _____ "This too shall pass" only works for me briefly.
B) _____ "This too shall pass," bedrock for how I live life.

FOLLOWING UP ON YOUR SCORES

1. Add up how many As and how many Bs you checked.
2. The feedback below is organized into three simple categories: problem solving, policies and procedures, and mindset control.
3. Review both descriptions and reflect on where you might be on the scale.

ANALYZING YOUR RESULTS

If you answered A to the majority of the questions:

In regard to problem solving, you may be someone who prefers to make decisions immediately and move forward. When confronted with a conflicting opinion, it may be an opportunity for you to engage others more directly. Essentially, you welcome the opportunity to defend your perspective with strong opinions. Conflict is OK with you.

As decisions are made, you may often find yourself possessing a strong desire to want to talk more about the surrounding circumstances and ramifications of an issue. You may possess a strong need to analyze these rules and want changes because you see components that are not working. In regard to taming your mind, you cannot turn the switch off. Oftentimes, your mind is racing (impacting sleep). You may have a tendency to fixate on various communication episodes or situations that take place and struggle to let them go. At home, in the car, on weekends, you may still be *living school* or a *personal life experience* inside your mind.

Within the dyadic relationship between teaching and learning, those who express this type of preference (category A) may favor a strict linear focus on how to move forward with decision making. Often, this type may also swim in solution mode and discover challenges in noting the fine details of problem solving. Others may find that you make decisions too quickly without thinking through the whole picture. You may feel you are simply sharing your opinion and engaging people with supportive measures to back up your thoughts.

If you answered B to the majority of the questions:

In regard to problem solving, you may be someone who prefers to make decisions based on the situation and surrounding circumstances that are given at that time. You may tend to be very aware of bias and do not base your decisions on personal opinions driven by dualistic lines of thinking (right, wrong). An aura of passivity is OK with you and does not cause you stress. Because you tend not to verbalize your thoughts, feelings, and perspectives in meetings, you create a mental space that allows for reflection instead of a need for immediate reaction. When confronted with a conflicting opinion other than your own, you pause and reflect before reacting. You feel that silence increases your percentage chances of de-escalating problems. You tend to avoid and are uncomfortable with conflict.

In regard to policies and procedures, you possess a very strong desire to let the chips fall where they may. As decisions are made, you find yourself simply accepting them as given templates that you choose not to debate about too often. Your attitude focuses more on your immediate tasks as opposed to worrying about the managerial and political aspects of procedures. As rules are established, you tend to accept the policy deliverables as simply part of your job to adhere to and not an opportunity to complain or dissect further.

In regard to taming your mind, you struggle to turn the switch off (much like category A), but you have the ability to do so at times. You adopt a viewpoint about situations and people that allows them to pass without judgment or critique. The situations and the actions of others are in the past, and you possess the ability to keep them there. At home, in the car, on weekends, you do think about Friday's e-mail/post (personal or professional) or Wednesday's conference, but it doesn't consume you. You work to create habits of the mind that are not linear in reference to problem solving.

Within the dyadic relationship between teaching and learning, those who express this type of preference (category B) favor flexibility toward problem solving as opposed to a concretized allegiance to your opinion and debating the rules and procedures for the school. Often, this type may also swim in process mode and discover challenges in reaching a consensus or desired solution. Others may find difficulty with this disposition, feeling that you can never make a decision. However, in your mind, you have an opinion about the circumstance, but you choose not to engage that opinion verbally because you feel, based on previous episodes, it will cause conflict. Offering your opinion, at times, is an opportunity for someone to judge you. Because of your personality preferences, you may see the expression of your opinion as a superfluous act because you will need to conform to the controlling personality in the end anyway to keep the system functioning.

Chapter One

School Mindset

The Brain and the Triangle

In order for you to become emotionally wedded to the concepts and behaviors discussed in this book, it is critical to understand some of the science behind the writing. Possessing some introductory information about the brain and a term called *neuroplasticity* will help you develop the emotional tools that are required to reframe how you might think and feel. Thus, for this opening chapter, you will learn more about how the brain and the neurons themselves work and how that learning can be applied to your daily thought process and into a growth mindset.

Each time you repeat a particular thought or action, you strengthen the connection between a set of brain cells. Repetition rewires the brain and creates habits of the mind. Neuroplasticity refers to the brain's ability to change and adapt as a result of one or more experiences. Your frontal lobes are the executive control center of the brain. The frontal lobes allow you to decide when (if at all) you are going to take action. They also play a significant role in your ability to focus on the positive experiences in life and how much you actually enjoy those stimulants. The prefrontal cortex is what helps you govern yourself around societal expectations. This area of the brain sets your expectations to conform to the masses and think about others.

Many middle school students, as many of you know, lack the maturing of the frontal lobes, which does not allow children in this age group to see beyond their own immediate wants and desires. In adults, if the frontal lobes were stunted at a young age and maturity was not fully developed, then social concerns may manifest themselves in adulthood. There may have been a critical incident or experience within the family growing up or with friends that forced an emotional/empathetic shutdown on the part of an individual.

In her article titled "Teaching Is Among the Top Three Most Stressed Occupations," Kaye Wiggins provides insight through the research done by Sir Cary Cooper, a professor of organizational psychology and health at the University of Manchester's business school. "Of all the occupations I've studied, teachers are in the top three most stressed occupations," Cooper stated. Whether you agree with this notion or not, it certainly begs the question: How do you rewire your brain to a better place? Is this possible?

If being an educator is considered one of the most stressful occupations, how do you move toward alleviating the stress, de-escalating your emotions for the better, and finding the joy you once possessed? For some, the joy has never left. They have found ways to cope, adapt, and focus on the good. For others, the journey of teaching and leading classrooms and buildings has taken a much different course—where job satisfaction has fallen victim to accountability measures, helicopter parenting, and an overall feeling of being overwhelmed.

After all these years, is your brain capable of actually changing? When you look at yourself in the classroom and the school, it is important to understand that sober negative emotions cause slower cognitive processing. Negative moods summon emotions. They can drive the classroom mindset into disarray where accountability and blame are displaced to others.

In his book *Soft-Wired: How the New Science of Brain Plasticity Can Change Your Life*, Dr. Michael Merzenich, who is a pioneer in brain plasticity research, lists ten core principles that must be understood for the brain to be reframed:

1. *Change is mostly limited to those situations in which the brain is in the mood for it*. If you are alert, on the ball, engaged, motivated, ready for action, the brain releases the neurochemicals necessary to enable brain change. When disengaged, inattentive, distracted, or doing something without thinking that requires no real effort, your neuroplastic switches are "off."
2. *The harder you try, the more you're motivated, the more alert you are, and the better (or worse) the potential outcome, the bigger the brain change.* If you're intensely focused on the task and really trying to master something for an important reason, the change experienced will be greater.
3. *What actually changes in the brain are the strengths of the connections of neurons that are engaged together, moment by moment, in time.* The more something is practiced, the more connections are changed and made to include all elements of the experience (sensory info, movement, cognitive patterns). You can think of it like a "master controller" being formed for that particular behavior, which allows it to be performed with remarkable facility and reliability over time.

4. *Learning-driven changes in connections increase cell-to-cell coopera-tion, which is crucial for increasing reliability.* Merzenich explains this by asking you to imagine the sound of a football stadium full of fans all clapping at random versus the same people clapping in unison. He explains, "The more powerfully coordinated your [nerve cell] teams are, the more powerful and more reliable their behavioral pro-ductions."

5. *The brain also strengthens its connections between teams of neurons representing separate moments of successive things that reliably oc-cur in serial time.* This allows your brain to predict what happens next and have a continuous "associative flow." Without this ability, your stream of consciousness would be reduced to "a series of separate, stagnating puddles," explains Merzenich.

6. *Initial changes are temporary.* Your brain first records the change, then determines whether it should make the change permanent or not. It only becomes permanent if your brain judges the experience to be fascinating or novel enough or if the behavioral outcome is important, good or bad.

7. *The brain is changed by internal mental rehearsal in the same ways and involving precisely the same processes that control changes achieved through interactions with the external world.* According to Merzenich, "You don't have to move an inch to drive positive plastic change in your brain. Your internal representations of things recalled from memory work just fine for progressive brain plasticity-based learning."

8. *Memory guides and controls most learning.* As you learn a new skill, your brain takes note of and remembers the good attempts, while discarding the not-so-good tries. Then it recalls the last good pass, makes incremental adjustments, and progressively improves.

9. *Every movement of learning provides a moment of opportunity for the brain to stabilize—and reduce the disruptive power of—potentially interfering backgrounds or "noise."* Each time your brain strengthens a connection to advance your mastery of a skill, it also weakens other connections of neurons that weren't used at that precise moment. This negative plastic brain change erases some of the irrelevant or interfer-ing activity in the brain.

10. *Brain plasticity is a two-way street; it is just as easy to generate negative changes as it is positive ones.* You have a "use it or lose it" brain. It's almost as easy to drive changes that impair memory and physical and mental abilities as it is to improve these things. Merze-nich says that older people are absolute masters at encouraging plastic brain change in the wrong direction.

In order to best process this information and apply it to the educator's mindset on a daily basis, it is important to break down these perspectives from Merzenich into steps that are easily understandable. Discussing neuroplasticity can be extremely complex if one is not versed in the field of brain research. However, establishing a theoretical understanding of how the brain functions for change is an important basis for building a resilient mindset.

Oftentimes in schools, teachers and administrators work in a reactive mode to a variety of situations involving students, teachers, and parents. Because this reactive mode becomes habitual, the brain can become disengaged or, as Merzenich stated, *do something without thinking*. In turn, the neuroplastic switches off (see figure 1.1).

In order to avoid these habitual tendencies as an educator, you must further develop a metacognitive perspective to your day. By focusing intently on the task of monitoring your self-talk and how you are thinking, you open the door to changing how you experience the job of teaching in the classroom or managing and leading the building. Essentially, this metacognitive habit of the mind is the basis of how you will learn to control and change your approach to a better lifestyle in the classroom and the school.

Let's look at the act of disciplining a student who misbehaves in the classroom as an example in reference to how the neurons of the brain respond. The brain reacts to the situation as it has before: relying on the past

How often you *think about how you think* dictates your emotional energy physically

Without a metacognitive point of view

You take actions without thinking through a process

You develop a compressed mentality= Stress and Anxiety

Figure 1.1.   How often you *think about how you think* dictates your emotional energy physically. Graphic produced using Keynote template by Todd Franklin

experiences that have worked. The teacher and administrator who have the ability to predict what happens next—and anticipate the ramifications and communication efforts that will take place prior to making the disciplinary decision—are the ones who succeed in what Merzenich mentions as a continuous associative flow. This allows all the puzzle pieces involved with disciplining a student to come together in a concise fashion, avoiding fragmenting the situation into separate moments where the actions of the teacher and the administrator are misaligned and messaging suffers.

Thinking about how you think is only going to be effective and habitual if it is applied to the stressors that a teacher and administrator are faced with on a daily basis. As you practice working through the stimulants that cause you stress and your reactive nature to their existence, it is important to understand that the brain takes each experience (of which there are a thousand a day) and decides if the new initiative or change request is worth trying to make permanent. As Merzenich mentions, "It only becomes permanent if your brain judges the experience to be novel enough" to want to stick. As you apply this brain functioning understanding to how you view the classroom and the school, remember what Merzenich stresses about the memory portion of the brain: "Memory guides and controls most learning." If you practice the concepts outlined in this book, you will *build habitual thought patterns that become more resilient to stress and pull you out of that funky mood that lasts for hours and minimizes the ruminating process.*

Working from this platform of principles of the brain by Merzenich, you should be asking yourself one question: now what? If you have had any prior experiences with learning about mindsets (growth and fixed), then you are familiar with the link between how your brain is wired and how you approach problems. How do you change the interpretations and behaviors that you have not liked about yourself, your teaching craft, your experiences on the job, or, if you are a school administrator, how you have governed the school? The answers to these questions and much more will operate off this prescribed platform about neuroplasticity. In this book, you will learn how you can control your mindset *while the stress of* that student, that parent, that colleague, or that family member is taking place.

- Successful teachers and administrators refrain from creating power struggles with rules, parents, colleagues, and, most importantly, themselves.
- Thoughts constantly flow through their mind; however, opinions, judgments, and labels about classroom responsibilities and school-wide initiatives are nothing more than passing moments. These solution-focused individuals refrain from complicating their problems.
- To stop power struggles, you must learn not to dissever the dynamics of a problem too much.

Dissevering your problems causes you to immediately close down your responsibility to your emotions and reactions. You may begin to blame other entities that are outside of your locus of control. By disengaging from your habitual mentality to triangulate a problem in the workplace, you develop a more open and competent approach to problem solving. When you become "hooked" by another's differing opinion, you are most susceptible to ruminating about the disagreement.

Highly motivated teachers and administrators do not allow their minds to adopt an argumentative mindset or brazen arrogance around a perceived injustice (e.g., these new initiatives are putting too much on my plate or these assessment demands are far too much). Again, it's very normal to initially have these feelings and interpretations, but successful individuals cease to empower these emotions by ruminating about them. Self-reflection is difficult because the process itself invites the problem back to you. You may feel you are not the cause or the problem. This may be true. Others may agree with you. But this does not fix your frustration. You are still aggravated, confused, and angry.

You may shift the responsibility of your emotional state back to parents, colleagues, family members, friends, administration, and central offices. This is easier and, unfortunately, can quickly become habitual. Codependency is also a concern. Once codependency becomes habitual, it becomes very, very difficult to see the need for yourself to change. Holding others accountable for your stress is a recipe for long-term dissatisfaction. It provides a temporary relief; however, it also excuses your responsibility to master your emotions for the better. If you are venting through texts, e-mail, phone calls, or online posting habits to the same individuals, you may very well be codependent.

By consistently looking to view the same classroom challenges with the same self-imposed monitoring system, you can, essentially, expect the same outcome each school year. Those teachers and administrators who embrace rudimentary and challenging issues with an eye on holding themselves more accountable for their feelings and decisions cease to streamline emotional responsibility back to the organizational systems that structure their day. Negative self-talk begins to concretize certain belief systems, which, in turn, inhibit your flexibility and growth potential. Those teachers and leaders who fall into this category should not be classified as people who are opposed to change or *resistors*. These individuals simply experience a great deal of comfort by imposing a specific set of interventions that subconsciously limits their ability to problem solve for themselves.

Due to the work of Stanford University professor of psychology Dr. Carol Dweck, and the studies that she conducted to build the platform for her book *Mindset: The New Psychology of Success*, rewiring our mindsets has now become, at the very least, a negotiable option. But how do you get there?

In her book, Dr. Dweck (2006) opens us up to the possibility of choosing and changing how we think. Her findings create a belief that intelligence is malleable and can be developed by looking at the differences between "growth mindsets" and "fixed mindsets." Individuals who possess a growth mindset focus on *the process of learning* and not on a final answer or image they are supposed to portray. Teachers and administrators with a growth mindset possess tools that can differentiate within seconds to meet the needs of students. For example, they don't become enmeshed into a misguided vision of *this is the gifted and talented class—no remediation required.*

As an example, from the administrative side:

- Growth mindset leaders do not become entrenched with cognitive ability scores from gifted and talented ability assessments where assumptions and conclusions may be made about a child, limiting their exposure to advanced programs.
- The more leaders can view their mindset *as a system of beliefs that guides their decision making*, the more skilled they will be at seeing opportunities in problems.

Individuals with a fixed mindset predetermine. They may argue with management using absolute lines of thinking. Fixed mindset individuals operate with a rigid disposition, viewing experiences with a judgmental eye on right/ wrong. When placing students in classes, for example, teachers and administrators who possess a fixed mindset rely on specific assessment scores to issue a yes or no vote to programs for students. Though raw scores are extremely important, individuals operating from a growth mindset view them as one entity in a much larger picture (see figure 1.2).

THE HURRICANE-GIANTS TRIANGLE

The symbol of a triangle is a strong representational pattern that clearly illustrates how to diagram problematic issues and reach solutions. The triangle serves as a model or anchor for teachers and administrators as they begin reframing their thought processes for the better. The triangle allows educators to mentally diagram their preconditioned responses to events and seek better solutions.

Oftentimes, in any school, these preconditioned responses dictate a circular mental dialogue. This mental gossip tends to dictate your feelings. It creates a disposition and, without recognition and constant management, leads to a feeling of being stuck. How do you get to the growth mindset described above?

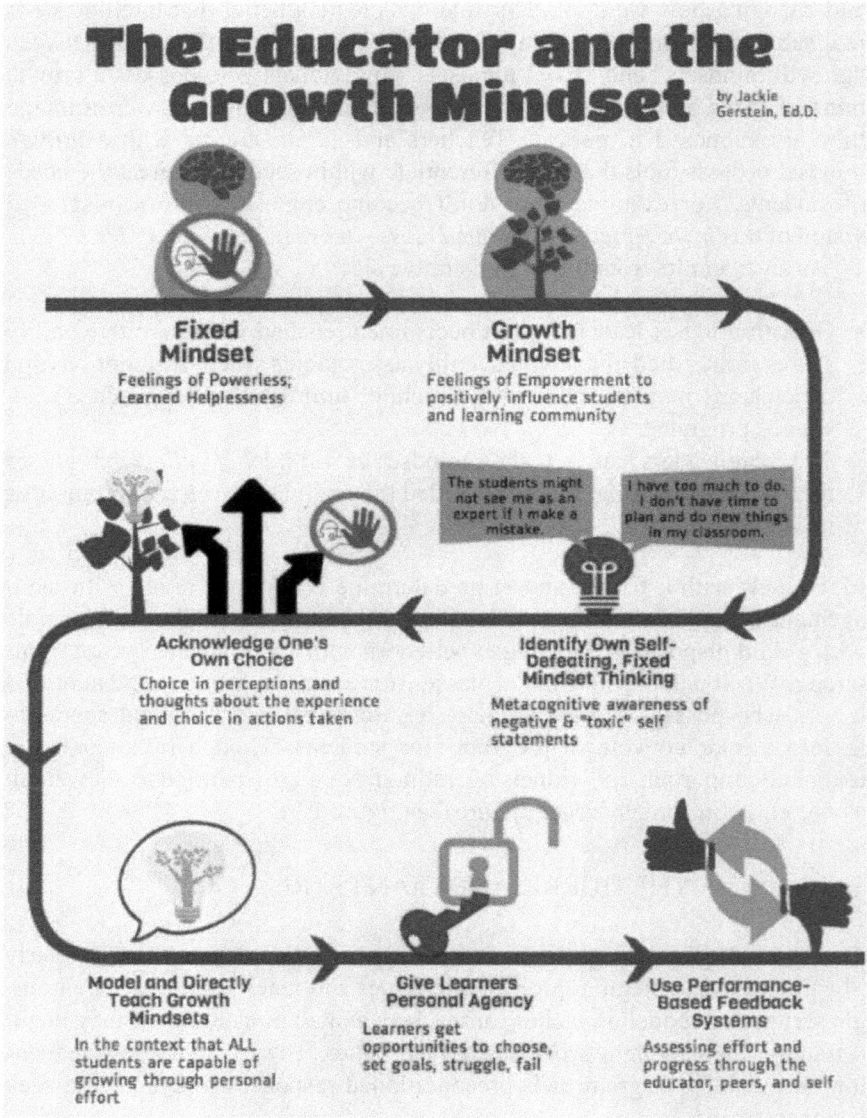

Figure 1.2.   The Educator and the Growth Mindset. Jackie Gerstein—User—General Education

The Hurricane-GIANTS triangle can serve as that solution. Any event you experience, on a daily basis, can be diagrammed through the mental image of a triangle. The events (right side of the triangle) cause feelings and interpretations (bottom line of the triangle), which cause you to adopt an attitude/disposition about the problem (dotted line left side of the triangle) (see figure 1.3). Challenges arise when you fail to develop a sense of *pausing* before reacting. In other words, once the act of judging a parent, colleague, boss, family member, or student begins, the triangles are complete (all lines solid) and your moods are hijacked.

You must recognize how quickly and how often this mental triangle forms on a daily basis. Thousands of experiences each day create thousands of feelings. They are instinctual, habitual, and oftentimes subconscious. However, the step that is often misunderstood and overlooked is the fact that you have a thousand chances to choose an attitude for the better. This line of the triangle (the attitude) is negotiable and is represented by a dotted line.

If you fail to see this attitude line as a negotiable entity, you will continue to drive an emotional wedge between your problem-solving ability and your emotional contentment. Over time, the inability to negotiate and break the third leg (attitude) becomes an engrained and unwanted habit, almost like an addiction to blaming another. The third line (attitude) is the only negotiable line that you can control. Stimulants for stress will always exist and feelings about those stimulants will always exist. These two lines of the triangle are concrete and non-negotiable (trigger and emotional reaction).

Triangles: How they work

| Stimulants | Emotions and Reactions | Create Opportunities to Reframe Your Attitude |

Figure 1.3.   Triangles: How They Work. Graphic by Todd Franklin

For example, the two solid entities of the triangle that you have no control over in schools are (a) the students that enter your classrooms and (b) the parents with whom you work to ensure each child's success. You must discover, through recognition, the attitude line is the only negotiable entity. Over time, with practice, the power of controlling this line becomes easier. You begin to notice that your habitual reactions to perceived injustices begin to soften and your mentality shifts from a blaming and complaining perspective to a more open platform that sees a bigger picture around the problem. Those closed reactions no longer become a common staple to your problem solving. Your feelings about the mistreatment from others or the desire to try and fix that parent, that colleague, that brother or that sister, and so forth lessen.

Solution Summary

- Repetition rewires the brain and creates habits of the mind.
- Monitor your self-talk.
- Successful teachers and administrators refrain from creating power struggles with rules, parents, colleagues, and, most importantly, themselves.
- View your mindset as a system of beliefs that guides your decision making.

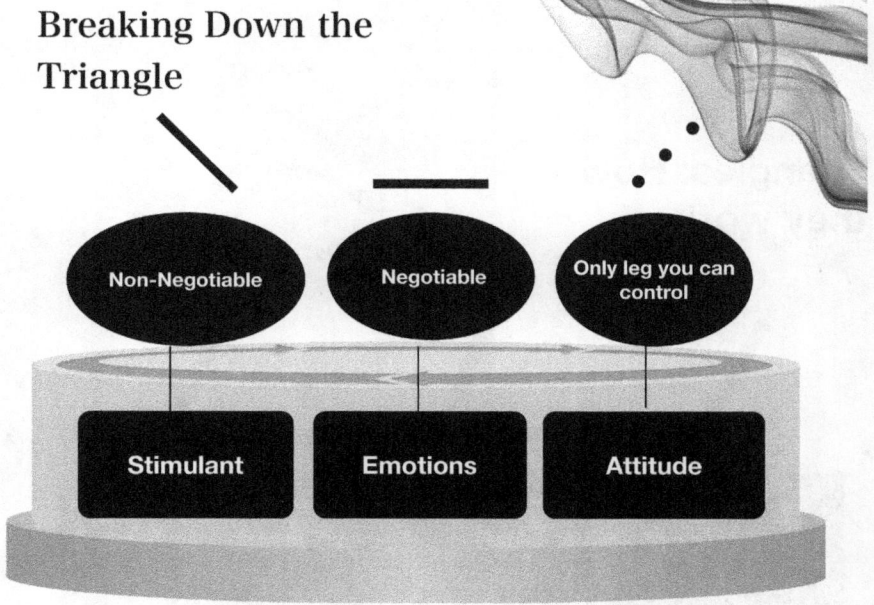

Figure 1.4.   Breaking Down the Triangle. Graphic by Todd Franklin

In order to accomplish these summary points, you want to apply the triangle concepts discussed as often as you can. Practice with the little experiences that are not that stressful but allow you to quickly diagram your thoughts.

It's okay to say to yourself, "Here is the stressor that is happening *right now* and here is my emotional reaction that I am feeling *right now*." Being able to change your internal voice to recognizing and identifying the two sides of the triangle (trigger and reaction) is a big step. This takes a lot of practice because you so often can become stuck bouncing back and forth between the stimulant and your reaction and never get to a thought process that looks to your current attitude and how to adjust it for the better.

Chapter Two

Professional Happiness

Anticipation Is the Key

In this chapter, you will learn more about the importance of re-establishing your habits of the mind and how the triangle concept for mindset solutions was created. Highly motivated educators set the table each morning for how they are going to approach and interpret the events of the day.

- They create the conditions for their personal experiences by anticipating problems but not judging their existence.
- The motivated and enthusiastic teachers and administrators avoid falling victim to the mental gymnastics of emotions that are sparked by an e-mail received or a decision that was made.
- Open-minded individuals find ways to avoid interpreting the roles they play each day with an exaggerated sense of importance.
- Learn to stay with today.

As they start their days, growth mindset individuals recognize uncomfortable sensations about their job, home life, or financial situations. They see these negative feelings as temporary visitors, just like a salesman at the front door. They know how to migrate back to a healthy baseline of emotional strength by cleansing the manner in which they fixate on negative issues.

On the flip side, prior to establishing a leadership role over their percep-tions in the school, a person possessing a more compressed mentality may interpret specific managerial and compliance issues as right or wrong (fair or unfair). Complaint-free individuals avoid this trap. They recognize that when they begin to blame or complain to others outwardly, they are the ones who are hurting themselves. Every day in a school setting, there are multiple chances for "things" to move in many directions. Your moods and reactions can resemble roller coasters. The belief that there is an alternative way of thinking about your problems can slow down the roller coaster.

The term *professional happiness* is subjective, unpredictable, and extremely difficult to quantify or maintain. However, if you look at studies that reflect the most common characteristics that lead to a more sustainable pattern of professional happiness, you can learn from the experts who have ironed out the possible solutions. According to Edward Deci and Richard Ryan, there are three psychological needs that motivate individuals: autonomy, competence, and relatedness. With the three needs being met, their studies show that people will initiate behavior that is essential to their well-being.

So how do school-based administrators apply these factors to their hardworking, dedicated classroom teachers? At the surface, a work environment laced with autonomy and creativity may seem difficult to sustain due to the increase in accountability for test scores. As is always the case, where is the time to allow for autonomy in our classrooms where project-based learning and flipped classrooms can live throughout many hallways of many schools? The answer is more obvious than you might think when you look back at your relationship with problem interpretation and problem solving.

In other words, look at what you have complained about repetitively each year. Is it class size? Is it parental input? Is it your colleagues on your team? Is it the teachers before you who did not teach _____ or the lack of administrative consequences? Many, if not everyone at some point, have fallen victim to these complaints. Yet every one of them is out of your control. You can't control the number of students assigned to your roster and you can't control administrative discipline. You can't control the parents who e-mail you daily. And you cannot control the colleagues you are assigned to work with.

- Your job is to stop identifying these issues as problems because there is no solution.
- You will gain the mental time back for creativity within your classroom and autonomy with how you teach by letting go of these cyclical stressors. You have no control over them from one year to the next, yet they have taken up a tremendous amount of parking space in your head.

This is a very challenging habit of the mind to tackle, but if mastered, it will expand your emotional competence and your ability to let things go. It cuts to the heart of really embracing the concept of wanting to change. In reality, you can *do better*. There is always room to excel more and so on. However, knowing that this is the case and actually taking action to improve is difficult. But is it really?

In their book, *Stress, Appraisal, and Coping*, Richard Lazarus and Susan Folkman fixate on a belief that stress is more about the interpretation of events and not the action itself. They believed that the transaction (the beginning of the event) occurs between a person and the environment. The stress results from an imbalance between demands and resources. They believed that you become stressed when the pressure exceeds the cognitive resources that you have available. Thus, it is your own interpretation (thought processes about the event), which happens in seconds, that is the driver for stress more so than the event itself.

The act of pushing yourself to reframe your approach to stress is difficult in the moment. However, it is you who can either take what you have been given, dwell on all that will mean for you during the school year, share your frustrations, and swim in the pool of ambiguity and stress; or you can work toward stretching your own cognitive dissonance and bridging that achievement gap between how you interpret and experience your emotions toward problems and the end result of your mood on a daily basis. You can do this by looking at the triangle concept and applying it to everyday events.

Becoming a wiser and more open individual means embracing the fact that more often than not, verbalizing your opinion, 90 percent of the time, is not changing the situation. In fact, it can strain relationships and add stress as opposed to alleviating its existence. To the egomaniacal individual, this philosophy is complacent and apathetic. To the self-actualized leader, this philosophy is a backbone for creating a bond with colleagues and the organization.

Complacency is a term, like *passivity*, that conjures up negative feelings and emotions. They are not appealing characteristics for most people. Advocating for complacency and passivity is not a good thing for leaders. However, knowing how to take a backseat effectively is recognizing your opinion is one, unilateral perspective. In order to accomplish this, *strategic* complacency and passivity can help.

As Susan David said in her book *Emotional Agility*, we constantly compare ourselves. She mentions that self-acceptance (sense of self and life satisfaction) "takes a big hit anytime we start making comparisons." She talks about getting hooked on external validation to prove your own sense of value.

In addition to this introspective look at how we may compare ourselves to one another far too consistently, from a broader perspective, David spoke to how various cultures define happiness. She talks about how, in North America, happiness tends to be defined by personal accomplishment, and in East Asia happiness is associated with social harmony. She sees the American culture being based on "socially disengaged emotions such as pride or anger." She shares how, in Japanese culture, happiness is based on loyalty. She believes that happiness is more "about how in sync your feelings are with that culture's definition of happiness" and that chasing after happiness can be self-defeating because of mood fluctuations.

However, David found that experiences like sadness, guilt, anger, or fear can encourage perseverance and, ironically, provide a more focused mindset. When you look at how you approach your classroom as a teacher or the school as an administrator, are you able to utilize negative emotions as positive drivers (or powers for good)? The emotional agility that David describes is a reminder to view your mindset with a sense of flexibility, like a rubber band that constantly stretches but never breaks.

CASE STUDY: ALEXIS

Understanding emotions are not fact is a difficult concept to grasp and requires this emotional agility previously discussed. All too often, we believe, our emotions drive how we feel. However, analytically, it is actually the thought that drives feelings. It is the preconditioned responses to typical events that drive your moods. As one assistant principal worked with a world history teacher, Alexis, during her seventh year in the profession, it was clear that she needed direction outside of the instructional arena. Alexis needed to learn how to view her surroundings through a different prism and use her emotions of anger and fear for a more positive mindset. Alexis wanted to improve her state of mind in the classroom, but she seemed to just let the students "get to her."

Her classroom environment was chaotic at times, and the students tended to drive the instructional climate. Alexis would consistently look for the responsibility of the chaos to be displaced elsewhere. Her thoughts centered on not receiving enough support from her administration or that the students just simply didn't care. The issue became pervasive because her mentality would spread into the culture of the staff in various arenas. During one meeting with her administrator, Alexis admitted that she wanted to feel better. She knew that her perspective was negative. She knew that others perceived this as well.

How does someone like Alexis get there and achieve a further sense of professional happiness? There were three steps to this solution that the assistant principal used to shift Alexis:

- Focus on fact and not how you are constantly feeling.
- Anticipate and limit the verbalization of your thoughts to others unless there is a solution that you are offering.
- See your current state of mind as temporary.

In their discussion, the two of them constantly went back to these three actions. The conversations helped Alexis establish mini goals for herself. They provided her with solutions, helping her not to traverse down a negative path. Joanne Ellison Rodgers, in her article "Go Forth in Anger," states that mild to moderate anger is an important and functional emotion. "Researchers are amassing evidence that anger is a potent form of social communication," says Rodgers. It tends to be "a logical part of people's emotional tool kit, an appetitive force that not only moves us toward what we want but fuels optimism, creative brainstorming, and problem solving by focusing mind and mood in highly refined ways." Using anger as a guide post can help us reset our moods. Instead of allowing it to grow and fester, we can step back and ask, *What is the real issue?* "Anger allows us to detect our own value in any conflicting interaction," says Rodgers. "It then motivates us to get others to rethink our positions, to pay a lot more attention to what it will cost us to get what we want—and whether it's worth the cost." Rodgers believes we shouldn't suppress it, but we should keep the flame low and use it to help solve problems and deal constructively with others. Learning to channel those frustrations in the classroom (and the inbox) can allow you to temper anger and use it as a reminding positive stimulant for change. Look at it this way: How have you used anger in the past? Has it really been helpful or simply created an enormous amount of anxiety and frustration?

With Alexis, essentially, her learning to apply the concept of a flipped mindset to the flipped classroom was an analogy that helped. The bedrock of the philosophy mirrors one another. With a flipped mindset, you are working on yourself away from the classroom. You are doing your homework on how you want your attitude to be for the next day, reflecting, learning, and becoming willing to apply the concepts in twenty-four hours.

The relationship is a constant cycle of learning at home and then applying your newly acquired knowledge, goals, and objectives back into your daily life. These are the types of analogies and symbols that each individual should create in order to engage their attitude for change. A book like this will never serve you the solutions you seek by simply reading the content. It is up to you to take the plunge.

For Alexis, and like many others, it is the mental work that she was willing to apply away from the classroom that determined how effective her changes would be. Her willingness to reframe her self-talk was a big step. She dared to think differently. Emotional competence, in relation to *on the job responsibilities*, is the level of understanding a person possesses in regards to the following: complaining about a policy or speaking without direction is neither productive nor resourceful to one's own mindset and those of others. A school law professor once provided the following advice to his class: Saying something when you have something to say and saying something to simply articulate a personal opinion and emotion are two completely different concepts.

The latter can sometimes create resentment with colleagues, breed the ingredients for a fixed mindset, and pave a road to blocking personal change for the better. Often times, those people saying something with no direction are begging for guidance but will be the first to provide a rebuttal to the expressed alternatives. It is sometimes important to detach from the reactions of others and their opinions about you. You need to act on what you know is best for the student and yourself.

In an article "Emotion Work and Psychological Well-Being," Dieter Zapf cited multiple studies on the relationship between emotion work and organizational problems. He defined emotion work as the quality of interactions between employees and clients and the "dealing with" aspect that comes with what emotional work demands. He concluded that there is sufficient evidence that exists where emotional dissonance is a stressor that is associated with emotional exhaustion and job dissatisfaction (Zapf, 2002). Clear communication, planning practices, and learning environments are equally important. These buzz words hold true not just for your classrooms, but with the classrooms of your mind as well.

In the example with Alexis, it was important for her to realize that she is responsible for providing herself with an emotional platform to succeed. These platforms are not extensions of educational forums. They need to be specific coping measures that build resiliency towards the challenges of the profession. Turning challenges into opportunities and ensuring your personal needs are met is a skill, not a statement or a quote to be posted. It is paramount for teachers and administrators to hone this emotional competence skill that nurtures the mindset with critical reflection as opposed to a blanket acceptance of the experiences someone else is authoring for you.

CASE STUDY: LORIANNE

Lorianne was in her seventh year of teaching ninth grade. The assistant principal asked her, "How do you do it, Lorianne?" She looked at the AP with a puzzled stare. "What do you mean?" she asked. "How do you carry on the responsibilities of such a demanding job and maintain a high level of positive energy?" Lorianne paused for a moment and then smiled and said, "It's about having real-time information. It's about being able to access your mental toolbox that can fix the mood that others try to bestow upon you at times. Without building your toolbox, you are left with a life of reactive states. Life will bring you many opportunities that beg for you to react. My job is to dig into my toolbox, pull out that monkey wrench, and fix it myself.

Otherwise, I will be waiting for that repair man to come visit me for years. It all starts with creating a visual."

Understanding the power of pictures is easy. Learning how to maintain a visual of how you want that toolbox to appear is much more difficult. Dr. Michael Mercer and Dr. Maryann Troiani discuss in their book, *Spontaneous Optimism*, how a key to creating optimistic approaches is based out of the recognition that you only have one thought at a time. You only can keep one thought in your head, and it should be based on what you want to accomplish and not on what you don't want (Mercer and Troiani 1998). The opening directions for building a positive mental toolbox begin with taking action. You need to want to change. Not having the ability to change is different from not wanting to change. School-based personnel who don't have the ability to change are not willing to look at themselves. Give yourself a gift and start looking at yourself today.

Some people are wedded to the status quo. The mere thought of changing is daunting. It is much easier to give away that responsibility to another teacher, parent, or administrator. Lorianne stated that the visual is the first piece of information she accesses. Once she has the picture of the actions she wants to take, the challenges begin. Anybody can paint a smile. The challenge is to reframe a bigger picture than today's problem.

It's not about convincing yourself. It's not about faking and making it. It's about keeping an anticipatory eye on the moments that can pull you out of the stimulant that shifted your mood originally. Lorianne was a cognitive coach as well. She spoke to many school district personnel about reframing one's mindset. Because of her background, the administrator discussed this Hurricane-GIANTS triangle concept with her to learn if she thought this was a far-fetched analogy or if she felt it held a sense of merit to her visualization toolbox.

Lorianne stated, "I see where you are going with it. The flexible line is the key. It needs to be taught. You have created the visual for people to better understand the mentality concept through the image of a triangle. But you need to continue to stress the 'how to' [dotted line; third leg of the triangle] and how to implement it effectively. You need to have a solution for people. Remember, if you are going to be successful with the application of this concept to educators, it must reach well beyond describing the pitfalls around the day-to-day life of the classroom. It must show people how to move away from their habitual tendencies."

Solution Summary

- Set the table each morning for how you are going to approach and interpret the events of the day.

- Blaming or complaining to others feels good for about five minutes, but your mood suffers for a much longer time. Understand this and stop complaining.
- Stop spending time on what others should be doing or on issues where you cannot solve the problem. If you can't change the policy of the school and you can't change the colleague or parent—move on.
- School-based personnel who don't have the ability to change are not willing to look at themselves.

Consistent professional happiness is not a fleeting thought that is unattainable if you are willing to change how you have previously governed your mental approach to the job. Much of your stress related to the job is centered on people. It may be a student, a parent, a colleague, or an e-mail that you received.

All of these stimulants can serve as stress, triggering your emotional state. You cannot control others. You cannot control how they act. And you cannot control how the administration sets forth policies and procedures. Thus, if you cannot influence the behaviors of others, you cannot fix the problem. In these cases, you must work with the dotted leg of the triangle and focus more on why you are allowing these uncontrollable entities to dominate your self-talk and negatively influence your mood.

Chapter Three

Emotional Pressurization and Your School Mindset

In this chapter, you will learn how, at times, some people may try to influence or control your behaviors. Learning how to recognize when this is happening and having the emotional tools to overcome those actions by another is critical to reestablishing a sense of control over your moods. Understanding how to preserve your autonomy and creativity in the classroom starts with navigating around those who are inhibiting that process.

Cabin pressurization is a process in which conditioned air is pumped into the cabin of an aircraft to create a safe and comfortable environment for passengers. Working with this analogy, it makes sense to view the classroom mind as an entity that needs to not just be nurtured but given new airwaves in order to reframe old patterns of behavior, creating a comfortable environment. The most opportune time to begin this process is in the summer.

Each profession has critical time frames for when the employees of a company can choose to take their game to the next level or stay within a more conservative domain of familiarity and predictability. At many different points of a given school year, teachers and school administrators pump out decisions (emotional pressurization) in order to adapt to the culture of the classrooms and the school itself. These new airwaves are needed oftentimes because the instructional climate needs to be revamped due to student academic performance, behavioral concerns, or community influence.

Emotional blackmail and *FOG* are terms that Susan Forward and Donna Frazier discuss in their book, *Emotional Blackmail: When the People in Your Life Use Fear, Obligation, and Guilt to Manipulate You*. This terminology is used to describe those people in your life that may be controlling you through the use of fear, obligation, or guilt (FOG). These controlling figures utilize these dynamics when one person in the dyad is trying to extricate themselves from the patterns or expectations of a controlling individual. Learning as much as you can about why people act the way they do is critical to understanding your surroundings. The term *blackmail* contains a sort of volatile and controlling perspective; yet the theory behind the fear, obligation, and guilt *drivers*—in relation to a person's decision making—can be quite informative.

Is there someone in your school who unilaterally is always bringing issues to the faculty advisory committee meetings or union representatives in order to push forward an individual agenda that could be discussed and solved at the school level; without advertising the issue for public consumption? Is there somebody in your personal or professional life that expects you to conform to the masses due to an obligatory team meeting or familial ritual that does not mesh with your experience or desire? Are you being controlled (or dragged along) by the expectations of another person's desire to please someone else?

Susan Forward describes how emotional blackmailers use FOG in their relationships to gain power. Oftentimes, these dynamics will manifest themselves through specific relationships. In the teaching and learning prism, there is a susceptibility for educators to succumb to the requests or demands of others because the profession by definition breeds that type of mentality: service industry. Closing your personal achievement gap is 100 percent about accepting the service industry mindset but reframing your attitude away from "If only things would change, I would feel differently."

Everyone in life has met, worked with, lived with, or befriended an emotional blackmailer. From a systems perspective, the "other" must conform to the desires of the controlling personality so the peace (albeit dysfunctional) is maintained. Each person stays in their prescribed role to avoid conflict and to maintain some sense of normalcy or contentment. The emotional blackmailer (in families, this may be the parents, and in schools, it may be the team leader) needs a subservient counterpart to make the system work.

Living well emotionally is a learned concept. Through much of the self-help literature and *better-our-life philosophies*, we establish a theoretical understanding of how we should be living our life, but we need to be more wedded, emotionally, to those postulates.

Over the working years, you will quickly discover there will be people in your life (colleagues and parents) who will try to "get their way" via accusatory e-mails (CC'd to the principal) or abrasive and direct communication.

CASE STUDY: TERESA

As Teresa, a social studies teacher, spoke with her administrator at a social event for school, she felt like she needed to explain more about why she was struggling at work. Though an uncomfortable interaction to have, Teresa wanted to explain why her job performance was not as exceptional as in years past. She expressed that her husband was an emotional blackmailer. She found herself losing the motivation and energy to come to work because of her home situation, and there was a coworker who possessed similar traits as her husband.

These types of conversations take place all too often in the work setting and are very personal, yet serve as a reminder of day-to-day living in the workplace. People tend to bond and build relationships with others and speak about *what is really happening* in their life. As educators, no matter what happens at home, the next morning, you put on the comforting, empathetic, and supportive hat for children—when perhaps it is you or a colleague who may need that support the most. As Teresa spoke about how her life at home was impacting her mindset on the job, she also realized she was living a dichotomous lifestyle: one person in the classroom and a very different person at home.

Teresa used to be a flight attendant. She stated that the process of always *looking the part* in front of others was a staple to one's success in the profession. However, she felt the job was never different. She felt it was the same responsibility day after day. Her creativity was stunted. Thus, she was brought to the field of teaching expecting a different experience. Some teachers, such as Teresa, say they want change, but they don't want to let go of the predictable comfort zones that exist on the job. They just kind of want the "other something" to change or the administration to fix it.

Teresa, like many people, would rather emotionally stay in her conceptual prism of not taking action instead of changing, truly changing, for the better. As she talked more with her administrator, she began to recognize that she didn't want to attack the disease, only complain about the symptoms. Individuals like Teresa have yet to learn the emotional skills to navigate uncomfortable feelings.

As an educator, concepts and analogies are what bring stories to life. They also serve as the gateway for change. The administrator explained to Teresa, "If you want to change, you have to accept one main given. You have to be willing to give up the way you have normally dealt with difficult people and situations." For Teresa, she wasn't able to change her husband or the coworker who was like him.

However, after talking through her problems, she tried the Hurricane-GIANTS (Getting Involved and Not Taking Sides) concept: cannot change husband (stimulant), cannot change coworker (stimulant), frustrated and an-

FOG Triangle for Teresa

Hurricane-GIANTS

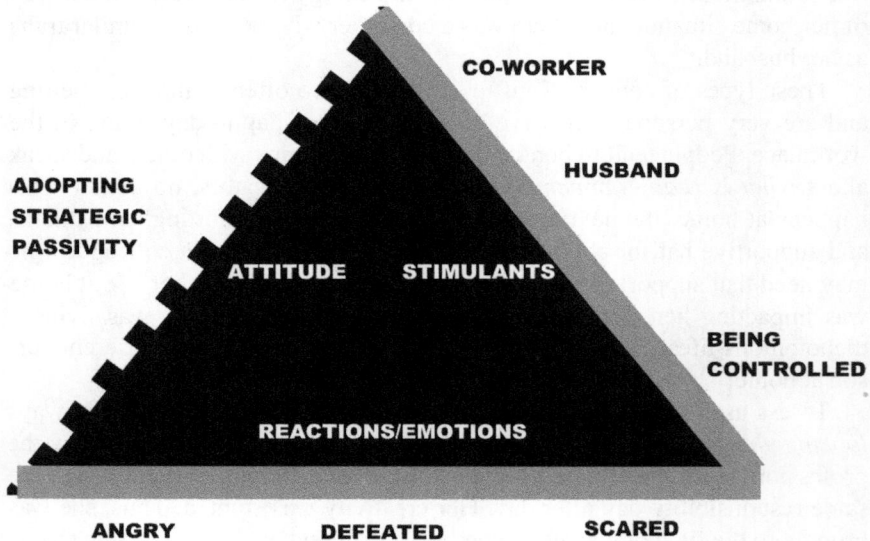

Figure 3.1.   FOG Triangle for Teresa. Graphic by Todd Franklin

gry and scared (emotional reaction), but could change her attitude (dotted line negotiable) by freeing herself of destructive thought patterns. She did this by (a) catching herself ruminating and (b) adopting strategic passivity.

Some people don't need this. Adopting strategic passivity around her controlling colleagues at school is what worked for Teresa, but it took lots of practice. For Teresa, by dropping the constant resistance to the emotional blackmailer, she was able to become more passive than confrontational. Strategic passivity requires you to defer your opinion at times. Emotional blackmailers cannot function unless they have control. They become irritable and oftentimes irrational with their reasoning in order to push forward their opinion. In short, it is more important for these individuals to feel right than to be happy.

In this case, Teresa knew her colleague (or husband) was not going to change. She also knew if she didn't adopt a more passive attitude toward some of the controlling ways these individuals deployed, her quality of life would suffer. Until you have been lying in bed at 2:15 a.m. fixating on the noun (that e-mail, that staff member, that parent, that family member) and then attempting to go to work, this concept may be difficult to grasp. When you drive to work or return home and possess an extraordinary amount of anxiety around another person, then you should know that you need to try something different.

Catching and recognizing "My life is in chaos right now, yet I have to teach" should be a personal red flag. It should also be comforting to know that *everybody* has this thought at some point. You are not alone. However, it should serve as a stimulant to shift your focus to concepts that will support you and allow you to view your problems more analytically as opposed to emotionally.

- The triangle concepts can, initially, help you establish that stable pressurization or mental pause that will drive you to stay more open.
- By practicing this mental diagramming, you can build a habit of resiliency where you are not fixating on the uncontrollable and focusing more on your own attitude.
- You can't control the perplexed individuals who try to manipulate you, but you can control your attitude.

As Daniel Pink states in his book *Drive*, "When the reward is the activity itself, deepening learning happens." Thus, you need a framework to create a deeper learning experience to help you see through your problems and not be stunted by them. Professional development or a book of the like should not be short on strategy specifics. Yet, there is not a list of solutions. There is no magic bullet, such as a symposium, that will change you. You have to take the action and practice what works. As Pink states, "To maximize enjoyment and productivity for 21st century work, we need to upgrade our thinking to include autonomy, mastery and purpose" (Pink 2009).

"Solving novel problems depends heavily on the intrinsic motivation principle of creativity. Flow happens in a moment; mastery unfolds over months, years, sometimes decades" (Pink 2009). You lose your sense of autonomy and purpose the moment you allow *the other* to impact your mood. There are innate psychological needs that are impacted every day for the better *and* for the worse. You are charged, as individuals, to recognize and nurture your own needs by not fixating on the ones who are trying to steal them away from you.

This particular book talks about triangles as a solution. The concepts ask you to see the framework in your head regularly by diagramming real-life examples. It is just a process to consider. By considering different prisms to view your problems, you increase your percentage chances of writing a different script and changing your attitude toward discomfort. The brain is novelty seeking by nature. A narrow range of exposure to anything will be habituated. Periodically, frustration can breed resentment over time because people are unclear as to how to *categorize and contain* their emotions on the job.

Many people were never taught a process for how to best navigate their feelings effectively simply because the self-help philosophies, on the job, are not seen as cost effective. As stated earlier, the term *mindfulness*, though intriguing, is oftentimes too abstract for consistent application. Everyday school personnel need a concrete philosophy that speaks to solutions that open the doors for emotional agility and flexibility.

Hurricane-GIANTS invites you to stop seeing yourself as a reactionary individual who always needs to meet the services of others by falling onto one side of the emotional scale. It is a tool for empowerment. If you begin the school year with an attitude of self-exploration and a willingness to learn, you can reframe your attitude for the better.

CASE STUDY: JOHN

John was a middle school English teacher who was fearful of making mistakes. He was a perfectionist. He was uncomfortable when asked to meet with parents or present to the staff. By nature, he was an introvert. John worked specifically on his negative self-talk over the years; however, he was never quite able to master this state.

For John, it started every morning before he checked his e-mail, while he was driving to work. He knew there would be problems waiting for him in the inbox. Part of the educational profession is that one must learn to be very reactive to e-mails. Parents are pulling at you with questions, administrators need you to support _____, and students are seeking clarification. John would dread opening his e-mails because they would, in his mind, put him in a defensive position at the beginning of the day. One of the first actions he was taking on the job each day was explaining, in writing, to a parent about a scenario where his actions or behaviors were being questioned.

The facts of the stories were often distorted and, depending on the e-mail recipients, painted John in a negative light to his colleagues or his superiors. John would then forward the e-mails to his administrators stating, "I am done with this parent, your turn now," or "Can you help me please?" He would also tell the administration that he does not have the time to deal with unreasonable parents. After experiencing years of frustration with this mindset, John spoke to the administrator about how to better handle these challenges internally, so he was not bringing them home. But how?

He began to try new patterns around how he would begin his day. First, he told his colleagues and his administrative staff upfront, at the beginning of the year, that he understood that e-mails can paint a very unique picture about people. He spoke to the fact that, in the educational profession, these e-mails at times can be a very reactive response from parents when all the facts of situations have not been disclosed. He asked his teammates and the administrative staff to understand those parameters about e-mailing and explained that he would call parents to engage in discussions as issues arose. This freed John, emotionally, from feeling insecure and defensive when he opened an e-mail CC'd to the principal or the superintendent. He wanted them to see the bigger picture and not overreact about who he was as a teacher or his practices in the classroom.

Watch yourself the next time a student problem occurs that causes you to perseverate on the lack of support from administration, parents, or colleagues. Why do you hold onto it for so long, ruminating for days? More than likely, you have been triggered by a noun (e-mail, phone call, random comments, comparing, etc.). This is where the answer needs to change. By expecting the assistant principal, another colleague, or anybody else to solve the situation, you have already made a mistake. They could help you. They may be the short-term solution for today's problem, but they are not the long-term solution for satisfaction on the job or in your professional relationships.

This particular year, John was determined to conquer the habit that was inhibiting him from experiencing joy on the job. He worked with trying to slow down the stressors that tried to impact his mood. By recognizing how often he was defining problems and then dwelling on their existence, he began to create that *voiced pause* in his head, allowing for some de-escalation. By slowing down the mental gossip and focusing on his thinking as the events were happening, John began to improve. Instructional insecurities that once burdened his school day began to dissipate. He became more confident both as a teacher and as a person.

In his book *The Energy Bus*, Jon Gordon speaks to being a chief energy officer (CEO) for yourself. He refers to energy as "the currency for personal and professional success today." He continues, "Emotional intelligence has a larger role in dictating that energy level" (Gordon 2007).

- As a teacher or administrator, you can learn from this philosophy—if you work on understanding the self-actualized steps to get there.
- Looking to the outside doesn't fix the inside.
- You need to communicate with difficult people who make difficult situations for you.

Don't say to yourself that you are not going to communicate with this parent or this colleague anymore. This philosophy never truly fixes your situation with that person and, in fact, can worsen your problem.

For administrators, when you receive e-mails that are questioning a staff member at your school, face-to-face discussions diffuse the anxiety for parents and the subordinates. You may need to provide classroom coverage for a few minutes so the conversation between you and the teacher can take place. Responding with an e-mail back to the teacher asking, "How did this happen?" or stating "Please come see me" puts the teacher, once again, in a defensive position. For John's administrator, this was a learning curve as well. Once they had this discussion and both of them saw how they were *escalating their stress* and *robbing themselves* of their ability to be their own CEOs, their situation and relationship improved.

- Having a conversation allows the administrator to garner a clear picture of the actions taken by the teacher, and a greater understanding between the two individuals can take place.
- The teacher must feel heard and respected.

Until that conversation can unfold face to face, the teacher is still operating in a prism of being disrespected and underappreciated. Until those feelings are dealt with, collaborative solutions are strained and the situation can escalate, unfavorably, for all parties involved.

Solution Summary

- Accept the service industry mindset, but reframe your attitude away from "If only things would change, I would feel differently."
- If you are stating or feeling like "My life is in chaos right now, yet I have to teach," this should be a personal red flag to try something different.
- By considering a different concept, like Hurricane-GIANTS, you increase your percentage chances of writing a different reactionary script to your problems.
- By slowing down the mental gossip, focusing on your thinking (metacognition), and recognizing the negative patterns, you can improve.

Recognize who the emotional blackmailers are in your life today. Who they are may change from one year to the next; however, you should be skilled at locating their behaviors. If you are in a personal or professional relationship with someone who is trying to control your decisions and squelch your creativity, then you need to develop the coping skills to deal with them. They are not going to change. It is up to you to move beyond the hope that they will. Thus, if you are teaching with them, do not let their disposition impact your mood for hours on end. They are who they are but rise above their actions by noting them for who they are. You will take a large step toward greater satisfaction in the schools if you learn how to *navigate around these individuals* as opposed to locking horns with them mentally each and every day.

Chapter Four

Adopting a Different View for School before September

Understanding how to change your view before the school year begins starts with building expectations. In this chapter, you will learn how highly successful educators conduct this process and what works best. You need to really know, intimately, how powerful your internal conversations are when September rolls around and you begin the school year: "I'm running late. I can't believe this person. Why do they always do this? I have to do this again." Sometimes, just stopping and recognizing the insanity of your thoughts is reason enough to try something different. As the school day starts, stress and anxiety can take priority.

Positive individuals *always* look toward embracing a belief that is centered on what really matters, not the minutes on the clock, a bell schedule, paper shortages, or the isolated opinions of one. Copiers and paper shortages are a serious concern because without them you struggle to prepare the lessons for the day. However, if you are allowing these concerns to make you extremely agitated, this is usually a sign of something else manifesting itself through broken copy machines and paper shortages.

The best part of being in education is that you always get to relive a second once in a lifetime with every student's footprint in your class-room.

- By reframing your approach to time, temperament, and problem interpretation, you will find more of the balance that you seek.
- Highly successful educators invite insecure thoughts as temporary guests—only allowing their stay for a very short period of time.

Between department meetings, parent conferences, grading issues, and so on, stress and patience levels are often tested. At times, some of your personal parenting and educational perspectives may be in conflict with the philosophies of others. With a compressed mentality, you feel the need to explain your opinions and justify your beliefs. In turn, you develop a sense of "I'm right." This automatically means you have adopted that another's opinion "is wrong." This is okay. Expressing how you feel is healthy.

- Be careful not to fall victim to *always acting* on your need to express opinions. This can be problematic.

This strong, unwavering will to express yourself is commendable to the masses of management and organizational hierarchy. However, this philosophy of expressing yourself *all the time* can create a sense of self that is attached to outcome. This attachment to results is the bloodline to a compressed mentality.

CASE STUDY: CHRISTINA

Christina had taught math for more than twenty-three years. She started out as a substitute teacher, put herself through graduate school, and earned her master's degree in administration. She decided to stay in the classroom and never transitioned to the next level of management. She was comfortable with where she was professionally; she had three children and was married to a patent attorney.

As the years passed in the classroom, Christina often found herself considering how much work she had on her plate compared to her colleagues. Unfortunately, she allowed these thoughts to turn into conversations in the hallways of the school. Christina was popular with the staff and served as the social committee chair, and each year, the parents often begged to have their children in her classroom. She was supported by her colleagues. She enjoyed a loving family and worked hard every day.

So how and why is a teacher like Christina unhappy?

Even after twenty-three years, Christina was open to trying something different. She just wanted to figure out why she seemed to become frustrated with certain entities of the job. More importantly, she confided to the administration that she, unjustifiably, held onto a certain level of resentment toward her colleagues. She felt they didn't seem to have as much to do as she did. Obviously, she knew they were extremely nice individuals and often spent time with many of them outside of school.

Over the years, some of them babysat her children and supported her through the eventual divorce. As often happens in schools, your colleagues become support platforms, best friends, advice givers, and day-by-day life coaches. This is natural. Younger teachers find veteran teachers to be like their quasi-parents. Veteran teachers view young teachers like their baby cubs. All that aside, however, Christina still possessed this deep-rooted sense of injustice when it came to work.

As Christina spoke about all of these harbored feelings, she touched upon a thought. She began to review how she started every single day. She talked to her administrator about her thought process the moment she rose out of bed, getting something to eat, driving to work, and so on. She soon discovered the key that would eventually help her establish a healthier attitude. In Christina's discussions with administration, she revealed that she had a constant voice of internal complaining from the moment she awoke. It was as if this voice in her head dictated one common command every morning: perseverate on the injustices of the job. The culture she was creating for her mindset was a wall of resistance. Much of her internal gossip was habitual and went unnoticed. In fact, she would talk to her colleagues about her perceived injustices from years past as if they had happened yesterday.

She struggled to let them go. As she recognized and monitored her initial thought patterns, Christina began to create personal challenges for herself. She would count how many times she ruminated about the past or compared herself to others. She began to catch herself.

- It is this act of catching yourself ruminating that serves as the stimulant for change.
- The more you disengage from these desires to complain, the easier it becomes to not allow the amygdala portion of the brain to conquer your emotional state.
- Highly motivated, self-actualized educators do not operate under a bevy of should statements (this is how something *should* exist, somebody *should* act, or a decision *should* be made).
- They eliminate the *should* mentality externally so they can create the space needed to feel better internally.

How often do you fixate on trying to change, convince, or influence other people like parents, coworkers, and family members? How often are you texting your opinions about others or judging the events at a school? The highly successful teachers and administrators think through the challenges by being open to changing their decision-making models as needed. This is like exercise for the brain. It retrains your typical interpretations about the stress others cause you. This is key to disassociating yourself from the anxiety you experience on the job.

There comes a certain point in time when you must learn how to commit to trying something different and adopt some managerial courage for yourself. Look for patterns in how you interpret problems. Some immediate solution steps to achieve the continued desired state are as follows:

- Probe for a different insight into your interpretation of problems. Do this by becoming more interested in the term *metacognition*, where you focus on *your thoughts* and not the responses or reactions from others or the contents of the problem itself.
- Look at your emotionality around conflict and assess your state of mind while it's happening.
- Remove an *absolute-minded* line of thinking such as right/wrong and should/should not.

In his video *Everyday Creativity*, Dewitt Jones, a photographer for *National Geographic*, speaks about the winds of your perspective. He talks about what it takes to get the best picture. He mentions that the actual decision for the picture that he is going to take is solely based on the lens. When you put a different lens on it, you get a different perspective. He states that most people don't realize that in a thirty-picture article in *National Geographic*, he has taken more than four hundred rolls of film to get thirty pictures. That is fourteen thousand shots. He states, "I'm not looking at the mistakes; I am trying to find the next right answer." So how can you look at issues in the school through different lenses as opposed to fixating on the problems with the same lens?

When making decisions about grades, measurable progress, and behavior, there needs to be a sense of removing an *absolute-minded* line of thinking. The compressed classroom mind is conflicted every school year in these situations. You need a break, but there is too much that needs to be done. How do you accomplish all that is in the inbox? Your thoughts oscillate back and forth between incomplete marks, D and F marks, and so on.

- Extensions are needed.
- There is so much that needs to be done.
- More communication is needed.

Some colleagues, students, and parents may not act the way you would like. They may change for a while, but their personality traits and disposition are not going to fade all together. Oftentimes, you may add story lines to the injustice that you feel. That is, you add meaning to the action you observed. This is a natural reaction for educated individuals to deploy. It helps make sense of the world of dialogue that surrounds your day-to-day interactions in a curriculum meeting, parent conference, and so forth.

Kerry Patterson and her colleagues, in their book *Crucial Conversations: Tools for Talking When Stakes Are High*, emphasize specifically how our mental dialogue works: "Just after we observe what others do and just before we feel some emotion about it, we tell ourselves a story. We add meaning to the action we observed. We make a guess at the motive driving the behavior. Why were they doing that? We also add judgment—is that good or bad? And then, based on these thoughts or stories, our body responds with an emotion" (Patterson et al. 2002).

When you find yourself using terms like "always" and "never," your emotional state may suffer. Even if some cases are true, and you are the one who is always counted upon to produce certain products or carry certain responsibilities (e.g., accepting the thirty-fifth student in your classroom), fixating on the injustice of the situation will further divide your emotions. There is a lack of cognitive maturity if you continue to fixate on intangibles that you cannot change (right side of the triangle) and get stuck in reaction mode (bottom line of the triangle) by blaming others; as opposed to reframing your attitude and mindset toward the discomfort (negotiable dotted line of the triangle).

Solution Summary

- Positive individuals always look toward embracing a belief that is centered on what really matters; not the minutes on the clock, a bell schedule, paper shortages, or the isolated opinions of one.
- Highly successful educators invite insecure thoughts as temporary guests, only allowing their stay for a very short period of time.
- Assess the quality of your thoughts as they are happening.
- Internal gossip is not being solution-focused.
- There is a lack of cognitive maturity if you continue to fixate on intangibles that you cannot change (right side of the triangle) and get stuck in reaction mode (bottom line of the triangle) by blaming others; as opposed to reframing your attitude and mindset toward the discomfort (negotiable dotted line of the triangle).

This chapter challenges you to conduct an intake of your internal thought processes. Understand how often your mind might utilize embellishing language that makes situations or experiences more daunting than they need to be. This is yet another habit of the mind to be wary of as you carve your pathway to changing your thought patterns for the better.

Chapter Five

Achieving That Balance in Schools

Listen to Your Self-Talk

Learning how to monitor your self-talk and reframe your mental dialogue for a more positive approach to the day is the focus of this chapter. On a daily basis, a lot of material needs to be covered and smaller windows of time exist. Todd and Beth Whitaker stress these points as well in their book *Teaching Matters: Motivating and Inspiring Yourself* (2002): "How can someone who is in the demanding role of a teacher, professor, principal, superintendent, department chair, team leader etc. . . . focus on his or herself? When is there time? Is there any way to do it at work?"

You can find ways to do this at work. However, it must begin with learning how to protect your time and create a balance. How do successful educators achieve this balance that many others seek? The answer is simple: they learn not to get pulled into the lanes of problems that others try to create for them.

CASE STUDY: CHERYL

One of the more challenging behavioral prisms that teachers and administrators are confronted with is the "rallying of the troops" philosophy for problem solving. In other words, if one individual teacher struggles with one particular student, he or she may call upon all of the others in order to collaborate for a team-wide intervention. This process *can be* very effective. However, if you are not careful, the relationships that others have built with the student may suffer. For example, on some occasions, the student may be misbehaving only in one classroom. There may be some incidents in other classes, but it may be an issue where one teacher has locked horns with the student. In this example, Cheryl was the teacher and she had some conflicts with a student. She asked for the support of her colleagues with this student; however, they were not experiencing the same difficulties.

Cheryl wanted to meet with the parents, but only if the rest of the team members were present. Cheryl was putting work on the plate of her colleagues. She was asking them to not only take time to have a conference but also to support her own perceived need to fix something. This then put the rest of the team in quite the quandary. Cheryl's teammates wanted to support her as both a colleague and a friend, but they did not create the same type of temperament and relationships Cheryl did with her students. In fact, they found, over the years, that Cheryl had these types of situations all too often and some believed it was Cheryl who was causing the issue.

The principal spoke with Cheryl. He told Cheryl that this type of unilateral desire and justification on Cheryl's part to fix an issue with a student intoxicated the culture of the team and the staff. As she engaged everyone else, in what was predominately the management concerns of her own, Cheryl experienced resentment from her colleagues. Cheryl wanted to establish a uniform behavioral management plan across the board.

Her colleagues were feeling obligated to change the culture they had created with the student in order to support the managerial concerns (flaws) of Cheryl. The other teachers then experienced a rebellious mentality from the student with whom they did not experience similar concerns. Once the student learned that the *rallying of the troops mentality* was being deployed and he was now on a behavioral plan and being sent to the office for infractions, he rebelled, as did his parents.

- Highly motivated instructors on teams implement mindset strategies that diffuse the problematic episodes as they are happening.
- They establish the norms up front, at the beginning of the school year. Unless the entire team feels strongly about the concerns of one student, the team *is not* going to implement policies that impact the learning cultures of other individual classrooms.

Some schools have rules where if a child misbehaves in gym, music, or any other elective, the teacher reports the incident to the classroom teacher or the team leader. The expectation is that these homeroom teachers will report the incident to the parents. This philosophy breeds frustration in the staff. If a child misbehaves in class, it is the responsibility of *that teacher*, regardless of the subject they teach, to inform the parents about the misbehaving. Under no circumstances should another teacher be relaying the incident.

It is paramount that the teacher who witnessed the incident, or in whose class the incident happened, call the parents. This open mentality, at the beginning of the year, allows for teachers to possess effective anticipatory skills about how issues are going to be resolved. With these types of rules in place, teachers and administrators can stop feeling overwhelmed about the classroom, assessment practices, and grading. As one teacher stated, "It helps to accept the givens that won't change."

Monitoring your self-talk in schools is an ongoing, never-ending process. It can take a long time to rewire and master your internal voice for the better. Life experiences breed wisdom. Wisdom is not a tangible something. Wisdom, in the schools, is the *Now What?*, the asset, the outcome or emotional reward to overcoming challenges. One can't seek it or achieve it. There is no switch that can be flipped. However, once you have it, you don't forget it.

- If you embrace and expect the unpredictability of the school day, you are more apt to discover solutions, as opposed to resisting the typical problems, with a healthier dialogue to yourself.

To improve this self-talk skill, it is important to understand what self-actualization really means to you. As Wiggins and McTighe discuss in their book, *Understanding by Design*, in daily life, it is critical to have skills that allow us to self-assess and self-regulate in order to reach beyond the immature mind. They stress the importance of understanding "how we think and why, and the relation between our preferred methods of learning and our understanding" (Wiggins and McTighe 1998).

The personal achievement gap, for the solution-focused educator, is the void that exists between the experiences/problems you have on the job and your response. By the time you categorize the issue as a problem, displace the blame, and then ruminate about the issue, it is too late. The gap is widening. Your emotions, at that point, are driving your mood. Your pedagogy is negatively impacted.

Oftentimes, when you have an insecure thought, it is based out of a belief system that attaches personal value and self-worth to the decision making of others. While working in the schools, if you can recognize how often you are comparing *your job vs. their job*, then you can begin to realize how futile this exercise can be in your journey for contentment. Comparison modes of thinking are destructive in any relationship at work and at home. Allowing the actions of another person to stimulate an unhealthy emotional response in your mind is almost unavoidable.

CASE STUDY: A SEVENTH-GRADE CROSS-DISCIPLINARY TEAM—TRYING TO INFLUENCE

A seventh-grade interdisciplinary team with four teachers was struggling to find the time to complete all of the required assessments while juggling other responsibilities. The new pacing guides coupled with a new principal were overwhelming. They wished they had more control over some of the changes happening in the school. They wanted to work hard. They wanted to complete what was required of them, but the lack of autonomy left them feeling bewildered and frustrated. The Hurricane-GIANTS triangle concept is easily applied to an example like this (see figure 5.1). Remember, most of the stimulants and reactions to the stressors above will occur annually and create those hurricanes of emotion. The key to solving these feelings is to deploy an approach where you are staying involved with your team but not taking sides with a high or low emotion.

In this example, the teachers had been feeling overwhelmed for quite some time. They wanted to adopt a new style of thinking about their problems. They knew they had to accept what they simply couldn't change in the school. Initially, starting a discussion around their current attitudes was al-

7ᵀᴴ GRADE TEAM TRIANGLE

Hurricane-GIANTS

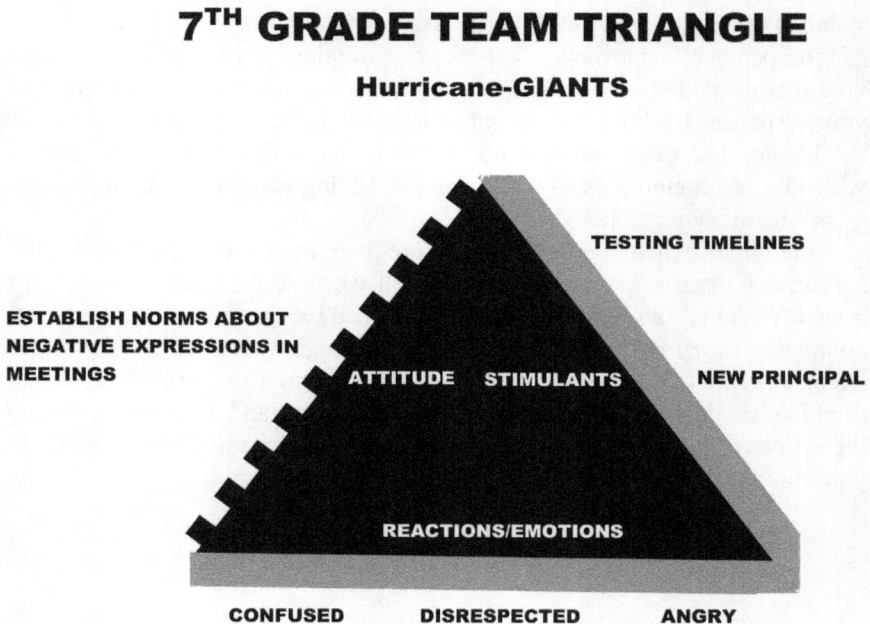

Figure 5.1.   Seventh-Grade Team. Graphic by Todd Franklin

most humorous. The sentiments were similar and the culture of the team was negative. However, they kept the goal of *trying to influence* the only piece they knew they had the power to change (attitude).

- Discussions about how each one was feeling about the concerns were the first step.
- Creating a new set of interpretations and behavioral patterns toward themselves and one another was a much larger and difficult goal to accomplish.

What quickly became apparent?

The high-energy, *willing to try and change* teachers (two of them on the team) had a different definition of what time and temperament meant to them. They established a focus that was distracted from tomorrow's lesson and appreciated more of whom and what they taught today. The work was completed and the timelines were met, without weeks and months of complaining about their challenges. Each time one of the team members expressed a negative emotion, the others would intervene by listening briefly, expressing empathy, and then moving forward. They felt more comfortable doing this now because they were able to reflect, within their own triangle of diagramming, and proceed without becoming hooked.

Kelly, a teacher on the team, wanted to improve the behavior of four students in her math class. She knew they were going to be a challenge from the first week of school. As October approached, her internal radar was proven correct. The students had begun to inhibit the learning of others. Kelly wanted them to be successful, but these four students seemed to engage one another too often. As the administrator, the team, and Kelly worked together to solve the issue, they wanted to discover how to break through the students' need to misbehave.

The teachers and the administrator wanted to uncover what was driving the choices the students were making. After many discussions, Kelly decided she needed to put the responsibility back onto the students. She had them make phone calls to their parents when the behavior reached a point for further intervention. In this manner, Kelly had the students explain their behaviors and articulate to their parents the amount of times Kelly had redirected their choices and the warning system and so on.

To say these four students produced a complete 180 on their behavior would be inaccurate. However, the immediacy of the phone calls and inviting the students to experience the anxiety-induced communication episode with their parents created a sense of pause for them. This sense of pause allowed Kelly to carry out her lessons with fewer interruptions. Phone calls were not the perfect solution that stopped the misbehaving students completely, but they created a personal bridge to the home, always a key to changing student behavior and providing you more emotional room for a growth mindset.

Solution Summary

- Don't get pulled into the lanes of problems that others try to create for you.
- As teams, establish norms at the beginning of the school year that address how not to derail your meetings.
- Don't hold another person accountable for the students you are teaching today. In the end, it doesn't matter how they got there or what should have happened or not happened. It is now your challenge and you can solve it. Otherwise, you will be chasing that same blame for years to come.

The personal achievement gap, for the solution-focused educator, is the void that exists between the experiences/problems you have on the job and your response. This line of thinking needs to be embedded into how you view and interpret your challenges every day. Simply thinking about how mad you are at somebody else or how disappointed you are in the decisions being made only invites unhappy and unfulfilled states of mind. Allow them to exist for a short period of time, but then learn to let them go by understanding, at a deeper level, that holding onto that frustration only hurts yourself.

Section II

Action Steps for Tackling the Compressed Mindset

Chapter Six

Reset Your Bar of Contentment at the Beginning of School

In this section, you will learn how to redraw your line of resistance where you can better address certain situations/stressors and alleviate the ruminating habit. You will learn how to truly confront your resistance to change and become more open to a different line of thinking. Resetting the bar of contentment means you are taking action that goes against the conventional wisdom you have accepted about yourself.

Almost everyone draws conclusions about themselves and people around them. The act of categorizing the personalities of people around you allows you to gain a greater understanding of your surroundings. Everyone possesses a unique window on how they view their lives. Some of those windows are transparent and some are only known to the eyes of the beholder. For the educator in a classroom and the administrator in the school, the key to discovering further contentment through the myriad of changes in responsibility and accountability is to constantly reflect on one question:

WHAT IS MY BAR OF CONTENTMENT?

The narratives attached to negative experiences can be rewritten if you understand the power of emotional agility. It requires a sense of quiet lucidity where challenging your beliefs around reframing a conditioned self is a tangible task to master; not lost in theory, not too abstract for understanding, and not just for others.

In 2011, the *Journal of Applied Psychology* published a research study on the effect of positive events at work on after-work fatigue. By looking at chronic social stressors, fatigue experiences, and the workplace, these researchers set out to discover patterns and connections with predicting levels of fatigue depending on the roller coaster of positive and negative experiences. Their study showed "that one cannot simply assume that, with regard to fatigue, negative events are negative and positive events are positive. Rather, they interact with one another and, with background conditions in terms of chronic stressors, interact in a rather complex way" (Gross et al. 2011).

Because of these unpredictable factors about what impacts your fatigue levels (work stress, student performance, e-mail interactions, family stress, online postings, health problems, financial concerns, etc.), you should embrace this as further evidence to move toward reframing your reactions to events as opposed to fixating on others (e.g., "I can't believe that person . . . "). By simply recognizing that difference, you can begin to change your mindset. Marriage, your profession, friendships, and the work environment are platforms for your personal growth.

If you continue to seek some sort of *personal happy* through these institutions or relationships, you will be challenged to achieve that goal. You are placing a large sense of your happiness into the hands of others.

- View your relationships (personal and professional) as teachable learning prisms.
- Don't always verbalize your opinion.
- Passivity is okay.

When you verbalize an opinion that contradicts another's viewpoint, oftentimes you adopt a defensive disposition. You are defending your opinion and, in a sense, subconsciously defending a sense of self (as is the other person). This is the recipe, in any type of relationship, for conflicts, arguments, and dysfunction. Because both parties typically feel strongly that their opinion *needs to be heard and respected or "is right,"* the Ego dominates the climate.

Some people may claim they are open to hearing why you disagree with their opinion, but their disposition and tone of their questioning communicates a message of inflexibility. He or she is actually looking to fight about why their opinion is better. It may be subconscious on their part, but it is why people tend to disagree. Arguments exist because each individual is trying to communicate why they are right and why *their belief needs to be followed* by the other party.

In these cases, some people choose to be silent, change the subject, or simply state, "Okay, I see your point." Passivity is not giving in to another person. Passivity is the bridge to minimizing the impact on your mood from opinionated colleagues, friends, and others in your life. If another person believes that being right is more important than keeping the peace within the dynamics of the relationship, you are going to be hard-pressed to change that concretized mentality.

Remember, you are looking to find answers that don't require change on the part of another individual (student, parent, family member) or an action from another (administrative intervention). Resetting the bar of contentment is about finding how you can take back emotional responsibility for your attitude and disposition. Initially, the concept is difficult to grasp, but with practice, the recognition of this concept becomes habitual and a different attitude, a more productive one, follows.

In order to effectively establish your bar of contentment, you must discover that intrinsic motivation for change. School leaders can help their staff with this process by providing a platform in the building that symbolizes self-discovery through a collaborative culture. If administrators operate from a top-down philosophy, change for the better will be difficult. Just like the teachers, the administrator must reflect on the small stuff: the individual conversations with people and their immediate reactions to others. It is here where the controlling/compressed mindset can manifest itself in covert ways. As a principal or assistant principal, your reactions to people will define your legacy. If teachers see your goals and objectives as politicized managerial efforts, intrinsic motivation is lost and staff culture suffers.

- Staff members need to learn how to break old thought patterns.
- Constant reflection will produce quicker results than codependent conversations within departments.

Reframing self-talk with positive motivational statements is not enough. Subordinates of the organization need to believe in the validity of the actions being required of them by their superiors. They need to see their own attitude and mindset as a tangible item that can be changed, not manipulated or measured.

CASE STUDY: TREVOR

Trevor was in his fifth year of teaching science. He sat down with his administrator to discuss some concerns. Trevor was an individual who constantly reviewed every angle to every problem before making any decisions. This was a strong asset to his instructional practice. His struggles surfaced when he led meetings. Because Trevor was extremely focused on hearing the opinions of everyone involved, the meetings ended without solutions. Trevor had become very frustrated and was criticizing his teammates.

As an intervention strategy, the administrator worked with Trevor on his group processing skills. Trevor tended to pass judgment about his colleagues and blamed others for his challenges daily. The assistant principal was able to guide Trevor's efforts while not suppressing the importance of ensuring everyone had a voice. The key to accomplishing this task was having Trevor maintain a two-fold focus prior to ending every curriculum team meeting:

• The last five minutes are for action plans without criticism.
• Give everyone a chance for a last word.

Not only did this method help his outcomes to the meetings, but it showed he was respecting everyone's time as well. Tendencies to pass judgment onto another's actions and their situations are habitual mental traps to avoid. Verbalizing criticism breeds frustration in the long term. The act itself causes you to resist school-based initiatives as opposed to embracing solutions around implementing them. Successful educators (both in the schools and the central office) maintain a motivated mentality by *not jumping into the lanes of others* with a belief that *these others* must change before anything can move forward.

   How do you interrupt this fixation on others needing to change before you can be content?

• You accept and expect to move on from perceived insulted feelings spawned from outsiders such as e-mails or contentious meetings.
• You practice emotional strategies that diffuse the problematic episodes by catching yourself ruminating for hours about how something should be (*according to you*).

This idea of not creating conflict with his colleagues required Trevor to accept a certain level of uncertainty about how he might have previously operated in the schools. As a teacher, if you find yourself blaming or becoming frustrated with students, colleagues, or the administration, then you have allowed the external to become the internal governor of your emotions. This is natural. Everyone justifies experiences on the job by looking at who is contributing to the problem. This shifting the blame, however, leaves you powerless to feel better on the job.

   The circumstances and obligations from one school year to the next generally are not going to fluctuate. You know how many students will be in your classroom, you understand the personalities of the staff, and you most likely know the culture of the community. Thus, the bedrock of your experiences from one year to the next is quite similar. Your emotions can oscillate in certain situations. This roller coaster, if you are not careful, can create a constant state of dissatisfaction. When things are going well, you want to keep it that way. When things are challenging, you crave the better. This fluctuation back and forth each day causes classroom stress.

As an administrator, if you find yourself blaming or becoming frustrated with teachers, parents, the front office, or the custodial staff, then you have also fallen victim to the outsiders causing personal stress. Remember, this is normal. It is the second leg of the triangle. Your emotional reactions (stressful feelings) will always be there. They are a constant. The key to overcoming these emotions is to limit your fixation on what you cannot control.

In *Managing Leadership Stress*, Bal, Campbell, and McDowell-Larsen discuss how often many leaders operate in a high-pressured environment and so, in turn, they are not able to recognize their negative responses to stress. "Because long-term consequences of stressful situations can be detrimental to your health and well-being, it is important that you identify when your reactions don't help alleviate the stress that you feel" (Bal, Campbell, and McDowell-Larsen 2008). Very motivated educators do not accept a compressed mentality for too long. As a change agent for yourself, you need to emotionally wed yourself to this understanding. You have to want to finally be honest with yourself and say, "Enough is enough. I'm ready to reset the bar of contentment."

A good example of this understanding, in practical application, is what Shinzen Young describes as working with a physical discomfort. As you practice your recognition of moments as opposed to simply reacting to them as they arise, then you create invaluable seconds of reflection that can stop the emotional hijacking of your mood. As Young mentions in the article titled "Five Ways to Know Yourself: An Introduction to Basic Mindfulness," "At some point, with constant effort and practice, you notice that even though the discomfort level itself has not changed, it somehow seems to bother you less. Upon investigation, you realize that you have spontaneously fallen into a state of gentle matter-of-factness. By being alert to this and exploring what that state is like, you are training your subconscious to produce that state more frequently" (Young 2011).

This type of reasoning and interpretation of emotional discomfort is extremely difficult to embrace without first really taking a look at the common question: do you really want to change? It's that simple. If you really believe you are stuck and you are willing to take a risk to change how you view problems as they arise, then you need to think outside of the box. This means you must be willing to admit that your current habits of your mind, at times, have worked against you. They may have served as the stimulants to your stress, not another noun, a most difficult lesson to believe and follow. Through these understandings and working with administrators, people like Trevor and others can reshape their habits of the mind.

Solution Summary

- View your relationships (personal and professional) as teachable learning prisms.
- Think outside the box with how you want to react to stress differently.
- Arguments exist because each individual is trying to communicate why they are right and why *their belief needs to be followed* by the other party.
- Passivity is the bridge to minimizing the impact on your mood from opinionated colleagues, friends, and others in your life.
- If you are struggling with stress, you might want to consider how your current habits of your mind, at times, have worked against you. They may have served as the stimulants to your stress, not another noun.

This was a chapter that had a strong focus on how to view your relationships as teachable prisms. Oftentimes, you may not always look at your personal or professional relationships as bridges to understand yourself further. The chapter also adopted a very blunt approach to how you might want to approach your attitude for change. It asked you to acknowledge, admit, and accept that your current, long-standing, engrained habits of the mind may be working against you. If you are able to look at your own thinking and avoid blaming, you are taking the first step to changing your attitude toward the discomforts that may exist in and outside of school.

Chapter Seven

Winning with Whys

Getting to the Root Cause of Your School Stress

Getting to the root cause of problems is a skill. In this chapter, you will learn a very effective method for how to get to the bottom of an issue. Before jumping into problem-solving schematics, however, you must understand how to outline specifically what is inhibiting your personal momentum. The ingredients to building a resilient mindset (growth mindset), one for the better, begins with understanding the simplicity of momentum.

CASE STUDY: REBECCA

At the end of the first quarter in her fourth year of teaching, Rebecca approached the principal to discuss her feelings of being stuck in the profession. She was feeling extremely overwhelmed with all of the responsibilities placed upon her craft and was seeking support. The principal, Maureen, sat down with Rebecca and spoke to her about accepting problems systematically.

In other words, Maureen asked the teacher, Rebecca, the following question: "What are the three problems that are dragging your moods down? In order to discover the answers, it helps to look at a specific number."

"What are the three constant negative thoughts or interpretations that are flowing through your mind right now? What noun is it (person, place, or thing?) What are you focusing on, from the moment you wake up, that is your momentum killer? Is it a parent's e-mail? Is it the administration? Is it the behavior of a student or colleague? Is it something at home?" she continued to ask.

The principal wanted Rebecca to outline these items and address their root causes. Addressing the root causes of your most common, emotionally debilitating issues is the first step to effective problem solving. In turn, the quality of your life, toward the nature of the job and how you view events in the future, can be impacted for the better. In their book, *Charting Your Course*, John G. Conyers and Robert Ewy share the story of a school district's journey toward continuous improvement while utilizing the Baldrige Award Criteria. One of the most successful solutions they discuss is the concept of using the five whys for root cause analysis and problem solving.

As she spoke with Rebecca, Maureen chose the school plan process as an example for how to use the five whys for root cause analysis. In this example of problem solving, the principal led her staff through a school plan development process by reviewing the data from behavioral infractions. The timing of this process was critical. In June, the perspectives from the teachers were recent and authentic. Once the concerns were outlined, the staff broke into small groups to review the behavioral data. The only two rules Maureen asked from the staff were:

- Use the word "why" five times.
- Never stop at the answer *because of the parents/home*. At times, this is where the root cause may exist; however, it is not something you can control.

Schools must work to control and create solutions that can be managed and assessed at the school level. If the teachers view work habits and organizational skills as a concern, this is how the *why problem-solving matrix* may appear:

- Students are not organized and do not turn in assignments. Why?
- They are not motivated and don't seem to care. Why?
- They do not want to take the time to show work and produce along the way. Why?
- Today's student is motivated by immediate gratification and final grades. Why?
- Their parents create that message. (Not allowed to use; ask why again.) Why?
- Because, as a school system, we have become too data driven with test scores. The message we send to students is that the final tests are all that matter. Why?

Because this is where we are in today's world of education.
So how do we change what we can?

This why exercise builds up the anticipatory skills of others. Discussions can then become more strategic and focus on what *you can do*. Conversations are no longer complaint-laced. Trivial issues cease to be debated. Accepting a greater understanding of big-picture issues allows schools to move forward and not fall victim to the paralysis-by-analysis syndrome.

In Rebecca's case, she narrowed her problems to two: e-mailing parents and finding time to plan for her struggling students. After talking with the principal about *the why approach* to problem solving, Rebecca went home and drilled down the whys to these two problems. She came back the next day to share with Maureen one of her diagrams:

- E-mailing parents is difficult. Why?
- Because I am not a good writer. Why?
- Because I say how I feel and it doesn't sound professional. Why?
- Because I was never taught how. Why?
- My parents . . . (Can't say the home.)

By not blaming her parents, Rebecca learned to take more responsibility for her problem. She accepted her issue as hers to fix. She learned to not perseverate on *how to write* the e-mail but, rather, to send a brief note asking the parent when a good time to call would be. This gave Rebecca a sense of relief as she was able to respond in an e-mail but not feel forced to explain, in detail, her perspectives and exploit her insecurity.

CASE STUDY: STEVE

Steve, a math teacher for nine years, was unable to keep his instructional team focused during their meetings. Their meetings always seem to derail themselves into complaint sessions. Steve felt that it was cathartic for he and his colleagues to vent and, therefore, Steve did not gatekeep the conversations very well. As Steve and his administrator worked to resolve this issue, it was apparent that something needed to change.

"We need a place to vent," he would utter. The administrator asked Steve, "How much do you think about the derailment prior to the meeting? Have you considered establishing norms?" "Yeah, yeah, yeah, we have done that and nobody ever follows them," Steve stated. The administrator then asked Steve, "Do you ever challenge your colleagues?" Steve pondered and paused. The assistant principal then asked Steve, "At the next meeting, when someone begins to derail the group, be direct and reestablish the task at hand. Tell the person that this is not going to be discussed right now; let's get back to the topic." Initially, Steve was uncomfortable being a leader in this manner. He felt that this type of redirection was the job of the administrator. However, Steve also recognized that, without a direct approach that confronted the hijacker, the meetings became resentful forums that lacked substance.

After many months of practicing his leadership disposition, Steve learned to take more control of the meetings with a keen eye on what Robert Spillane, a former superintendent for Fairfax County Public Schools, calls *keeping the main thing the main thing*. He became more comfortable with catching the derailment and not letting the off-task behaviors of one individual intoxicate the instructional forum needed to address the needs of students. He adhered to the following formula in his meetings:

- Don't allow yourself to become frustrated over individual philosophies that contradict *your way of living* in the classroom.
- Avoid focusing too much on items that will not relate to the immediate needs of students.
- Embrace the procedures for the school year as a given template. Once accepted, tendencies to judge the current status of the policies as anything more than rules to follow can be eliminated.
- Analysis and critique oftentimes, ironically, give birth to stress and anxiety.

In his book, *The Happiness Hypothesis*, Jonathan Haidt, a University of Virginia psychologist, used an analogy to best describe the conventional wisdom in psychology about the brain possessing two independent systems at work simultaneously. He described our emotional side as an elephant and the rational side as the rider of the elephant. Thus, the rider is the one who holds the reins and seemingly is making the decisions. In the educational setting, the rider, at the surface, seems to be the one in control of how and why you make certain choices around your classroom and your school.

However, as you look deeper into this analogy, in fact it is the elephant, in times of stress, confusion, and disagreement, that wins. The elephant (your emotional side) is much bigger then the rider; hence, inactions, such as procrastination, complaining without direction, allowing e-mails to shift your moods, are all examples of the elephant gaining control over your rational side of thinking and clouding your ability to improve in and outside of the classroom.

In their book, *Switch*, a *New York Times* best seller, Chip and Dan Heath discuss finding the bright spots as a stimulant or road map for change: "Investigate what's working and clone it." These are the types of small directional cues that educators can look for in their schools. Who are these individuals who have it together in some areas? Nobody has it all together, even those who claim they do.

But you know yourself.

PROCEDURES TRIANGLE

Hurricane-GIANTS

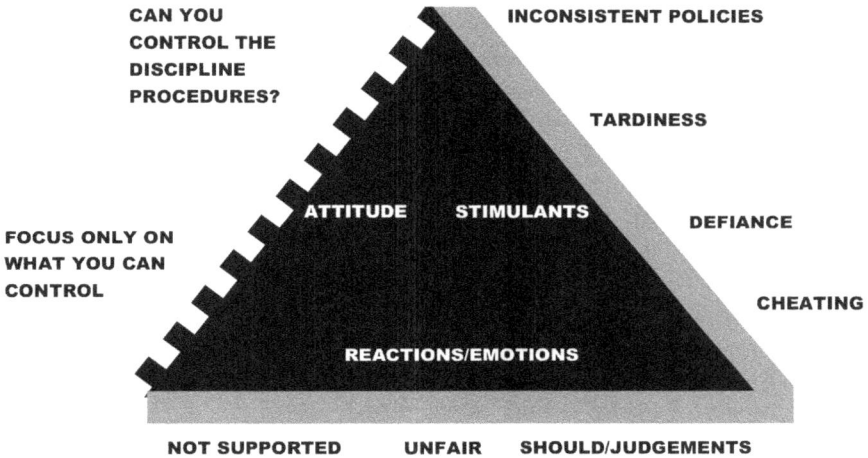

CAN YOU CONTROL THE DISCIPLINE PROCEDURES?

INCONSISTENT POLICIES

TARDINESS

ATTITUDE STIMULANTS

DEFIANCE

FOCUS ONLY ON WHAT YOU CAN CONTROL

CHEATING

REACTIONS/EMOTIONS

NOT SUPPORTED   UNFAIR   SHOULD/JUDGEMENTS

Figure 7.1.   Procedures Triangle. Graphic by Todd Franklin

You know exactly how you feel inside and what you really want to change about your approach to school, family, friends, and life in general. Traditionally, perhaps your ability to recognize what needs to happen has been followed up with your blueprint for solutions: the circumstances (people, places, and things) need to change. There is the trap. The colleagues at work who are frustrating you and the family members who irritate you—have they really changed? After all these years, do you continue to find yourself frustrated with the fourth-grade teacher or your sister, uncle, brother, and so on?

These thoughts of others needing to change are the misguided directions from the rider. It is the emotions from your elephant that need tending to the most (and, in actuality, need some tough love). As the Heaths point out, "The Rider has many strengths; however, a weakness is the tendency to spin his wheels. The Rider loves to contemplate and analyze, and, making matters worse, his analysis is almost always directed at problems rather than at bright spots" (Heath and Heath 2010). How do educators break free from the comforts of familiarity and the rider's procrastination and truly take steps to change how they think, the classroom mind? How often do you live with an undercurrent of dissatisfaction, possessing a desire for something to change or be modified? Social conditioning plays a very large role with your present-day mindset, mostly closed vs. mostly open.

The more cups of reflection teachers and administrators can consume in their classrooms (recognizing the elephant/rider relationship), the more their mentality can change for the better. At times, the actions or mandates of another entity can cause a great deal of stress and anxiety. Oftentimes, people may want to assign reasons to their feelings because their sense of contentment is being challenged and, as educated individuals, they want to justify and explain why those feelings exist. This is an educated and constructive habit that can serve you well. However, constant and continuous blaming of entities outside of your control can also become a habit.

Solution Summary

- Focus on the three constant negative thoughts or interpretations that are flowing through your mind right now. What noun is it (person, place, or thing?) What are you focusing on, from the moment you wake up, that is your momentum killer?
- Use the word "why" five times when problem solving.
- Never stop at the answer *because of the parents/home*.
- The brain possesses two independent systems at work simultaneously. Your emotional side can be considered the elephant and the rational side as the rider of the elephant.

This chapter dealt with specific problem-solving techniques on the job for both teachers and administrators. Using the five why solution to get to a root cause analysis for school-based personnel allows for strategic discussions to take place about problems and solutions that you can control. It forces the teams and staff to unpack issues in and around items that they can control or at least try to influence.

In addition to the problem-solving portion, this chapter begged the reader to view their brain through the prism of riding on an elephant. Understanding how you rationalize problems with the analytical portion of your brain while juggling the emotional consequences of your decisions is a gateway to discovering a more methodical and well-thought-out solution to your concerns. Building this habit only serves to foster more of a growth mindset in and around the school day.

Chapter Eight

Focusing vs. Fixating in Schools

In this chapter, you will learn the difference between fixating on your problems and focusing on your problems. Fixation and focusing are two very different concepts to problem solving and must be clearly defined.

CASE STUDY: VICTORIA

At a professional development workshop in North Carolina, Victoria, the English department chair, and Debra, her principal, were presenting together. Debra was telling a story about how, in six short months, Victoria had positively impacted her entire staff. During her second year as a school-based administrator, Debra hired Victoria from Texas. Her school needed a high-energy individual who had experience in the classroom and who could teach reading. Victoria started in September. By December, she was the English department chair and leading multiple teams.

Victoria was organized, possessed constructive anticipatory skills, and had a fabulous disposition with students, parents, and teachers. Victoria graciously offered her time consistently after school, led three different committees, and always seemed to have a smile on her face. One afternoon, after their monthly faculty meeting, Victoria approached Debra about some challenges she was facing with the personalities of some other teachers in the building. Victoria needed help.

Fixating vs. Focusing

Victoria spoke about what she believed to be the importance of recognizing the difference between fixating vs. focusing. First, instead of fixating on the challenging behaviors around her in the school (the rider), she believed the staff needed to focus more on the quality of their own internal conversations (the elephant). Fixating on a problem is the ability for a person to ruminate consistently about an issue without finding solutions. Focusing on a problem is the ability to hone in on the issue, not complain about its existence, and solve it. The educators who are most successful at what they do master the focus technique and don't surround themselves with people who fixate. By focusing, instead of fixating, Victoria watched the conversations change.

- Through daily recognition of how their old way of thinking intoxicated their current state of mind, the teachers began to recognize derailment and nay-sayers openly and in a safe manner.
- Those teachers who focused more on the systemic side of the problems, as opposed to their feelings about its existence, found solutions more quickly.

As Victoria discussed, working with the underlying existence of resentment that some staff members had with administration, parents, students, and so forth allowed for a more open and honest communication platform to solve problems. Victoria believed, if you subscribe to the fact that you cannot change other people who make the rules for you, it becomes obvious that your focus should be on your own thought patterns, mental traps, and reactionary choices.

Changing what you never thought you could change is a challenge. However, the idea that yes, there is another method you can choose to improve the quality of your professional experiences sparked an emotional shift, for the better, with the staff. By getting the staff to review how they processed instructional problems with students or grading issues with parents, Victoria got them to stop turning the same twenty-year-old reactive key, which only opened doors titled lack of support or lack of follow-through from administration or the home as the issue.

Once you stop fixating on how much there is to accomplish in and outside of the classroom, you can develop a more focused habit to your day. By reflecting on, instead of reacting to, challenges in the school, educators can establish a healthier temperament that breeds quicker solutions.

CASE STUDY: BRIAN

As Brian, a science teacher, worked with his administrator on the idea of problem solving, they both came to a very unique realization. Brian possessed a very reactive approach to problem solving. When he worked with students and parents, he was always solution-focused. His strengths were sometimes his weakness. Due to his nature of wanting to solve problems quickly, Brian would find himself stressed and irritable during those times when problems became more complex and involved the assistance of others. He would feel bogged down and overwhelmed. Brian struggled to slow down. E-mails from parents that questioned some of his grading practices or requested extensions triggered his emotional state. He wanted to solve the problems with the students.

The political responsibilities of having to communicate his decisions at every turn with the parents transitioned his emotional state into judgmental mode. As the assistant principal worked with Brian, they both developed a game plan that focused more on *upfront work*. In other words, they worked on advertising assignment dates weekly, makeups, and providing further opportunities for students to be successful. In turn, the e-mails and requests about the logistics of his classroom assignments and grading decreased. Brian felt happier on the job and had more time to focus on what he loved the most: teaching students.

But how did he, specifically, accomplish this transition?

- *Removing*: By removing his emotions from those late-night e-mails, which he interpreted as sometimes demeaning to his character, Brian was able to relinquish the desire to write back. Brian had to work for months on changing how he internally reacted to e-mails from parents or comments from colleagues. Ironically, Brian was a very calm and passive individual to the outsider. It was the internal turmoil that Brian would create for himself that was debilitating his energy, motivation, and focus. He had to learn to interrupt his usual habits of the mind.
- *Reflection*: He reflected more often as opposed to reacting. The act of reflecting more on his habits became a gateway to a healthier frame of mind for Brian. It wasn't an overnight fix. However, Brian's emotions were not as easily triggered. Brian also practiced not staying in reactive mode. By staying in a reactive mode in the classroom, Brian now recognized the why behind his struggles. As students misbehaved and interrupted the flow of the lesson, it became imperative for Brian to respond to them but not overreact. In fact, reacting without thinking is a recipe for further stress and anxiety.
- *Foresight wisdom* is a critical skill to develop. It almost seems a bit underrated in the field of self-improvement. Foresight wisdom is another way to describe the following thought/inquiry: Will I be embarrassed of the reaction I am about to exhibit or write in an e-mail months or years from now?

Brian had to learn not to perseverate on noninstructional issues. A misguided focus that is solely based on managerial concerns invites more complexity to simplistic and solvable issues. Though Brian experienced a state of instructional uncertainty by adopting this philosophy, with practice, he exposed himself to the possibility of reframing his behavioral management toolbox by not holding on to rules that created battles with students or parents. He exercised discipline but did not allow himself to become stuck with a student on the principle or spirit of the gum-chewing rule and just moved forward to bigger issues.

In closing, Brian's assistant principal spoke, at the end of the year, about an interesting analogy that stuck with both of them for a very long time. "Thoughts are like weeds," his assistant principal muttered. "They proliferate the landscape of our mind and require us to constantly readdress their existence if we want a healthier place to grow."

Solution Summary

- Fixating on a problem is the ability for a person to ruminate consistently about an issue without finding solutions. Focusing on a problem is the ability to hone in on the issue, not complain about its existence, and solve it.
- Those educators who focus more on the systemic side of the problems, as opposed to their feelings about its existence, tend to have a more positive approach to their day.
- By reflecting, instead of reacting, to challenges in the school, educators can establish a healthier temperament that breeds quicker solutions.
- Foresight wisdom: Will I be embarrassed, at some point later, of the e-mail I am about to send or the conversation I am about to have?

This chapter lays the foundation for how to view problem solving through a prism of focusing as opposed to fixating. It can help to use other people in the school as models for how to best approach your day. Find those individuals who are methodical in both mind and approach to problems in the classroom. They have an even balance or a strong sense of big-picture understanding. These are the individuals you want to pattern yourself after as you work toward finding more of an open and flexible mentality to the stressors of the day.

Chapter Nine

Remove Your School Sandbags and Become Your Own Innovator

Aside from the many mindset strategies discussed in this book about how to reframe your mental approach to problem solving, your ability to work proactively at becoming your own innovator is key to your success. In this chapter, you will learn how to foster an innovative mindset for yourself by exploring, experimenting, and rediscovering the idea of play.

At times, you may operate with an exaggerated sense of urgency toward issues that take you away from teaching and learning. For educators, many of the responsibilities during a lesson or during a discipline conference beg for a focus unrelated to instruction, such as behavioral issues, e-mail, and so on. For administrators, the myriad of educational initiatives and accountability pieces of the job beg for a focus that stretches their scope of obligations well beyond the primary task of leading a building. Stress is natural. Unfortunately, it often defines your mental positions. Because of this issue, healthier choices are difficult to locate throughout a given work day. Your internal dialogue needs to shift.

Because you work with students all day, naturally you are thirsty to talk to adults. Typically, when speaking to a colleague about your school day, it's very easy to take advantage of this time and express your frustrations. This helps for about five minutes but breeds resentment and discontent for a much longer time. The keys to minimizing these negative expressions are to

- Recognize you are doing it, stop, and then choose another path. These expressions rarely change the circumstances for the better.
- Stop thinking about "what if" situations.

- Observe others in the building. Using others as a benchmark *for how not to perceive or act in* specific situations allows you to have a blueprint for acting more strategically.

Stuart Brown—a medical doctor, psychiatrist, clinical researcher, and the founder of the National Institute of Play—has studied human behavior for many years. He is the author of the national best seller *Play: How It Shapes the Brain, Opens the Imagination, and Invigorates the Soul.* In the book, he states that people have a dominant mode of play that falls into specific categories. Based on his research, Brown believed that each person possesses a play personality and, as adults, we can lose sight of what brought us that energy or unencumbered sense of joy.

In the case of school personnel and the analogies drawn from Brown's conclusion that people adopt certain dispositions around their work, one may want to consider these characteristics at a deeper level. According to Brown, those individuals who fall into a play personality that is based on flexibility, imagination, and movement may find their mindset more flexible and not as concretized as others. These kinesthetic individuals do not need predictability or see situations as win/lose (Brown 2009).

CASE STUDY: GINNY

Ginny was an eighth-grade math teacher who was married and had six children all under the age of ten. Each morning Ginny would pull herself into work with a coffee mug and a banana.

> The teacher who communicates expectations clearly ensures a supportive learning environment. The challenge resides in creating clear expectations for oneself prior to walking into the school building at 6:47 a.m.

By the time first block started, Ginny had students engaged with one another, moving around the room, and loving math. She was the conductor in the middle of it all. The principal struggled to understand how she could produce these concerts in her classroom. How was she able to make that transition from extreme lethargy to engaging instructor? "Sandbags," she stated. "It's all about removing your sandbags."

The principal knew the analogy of sandbags as a symbol of fatigue. Not to his surprise, Ginny referred to the sandbags under her eyes as the reminders of attitude reframing. She knew they were there. She knew she was exhausted. She knew that the day ahead of her was going to be very challenging. "I can't remove the physical appearance of sandbags under my eyes, but

I can remove the internal roadblocks that they try to create with my attitude toward the events of the day. There are two sandbags which symbolize, in my mind, the power of choice. I can either choose to be exhausted, a sleep-deprived zombie that plunges through the day or I can choose sandbag #2. I choose #2 where I can move around and joke with my kids through drama and imagination."

Some people just get it and others just want to wallow in it. What is the difference? The administrator asked Ginny how she managed to constantly cut through the red tape and get to what matters most. Ginny mentioned that she understood the game: "I know management, at any level and in any organization, has actions they need to require from the subordinates. I also know that immediate action from a subordinate in reference to tasks issued = my boss need not worry about me or that department. It becomes a win-win for me."

Ginny continued, "I quickly discovered, in this profession, that those colleagues of mine that wait, stop, and complain are the same individuals who create complexity around managerial tasks. They then complain about not having enough time for instructional endeavors. Until my colleagues in this boat learn to make deadlines a positive bump in the road, administrators will always be dealing with them, the same 5 percent."

The highly focused and reflective educator's mind works to create opportunities every day where reflection is the norm, not the exception. Ginny and teachers like her understand how to use reflection to their advantage. They understand, completely, how to locate the obligatory task not related to students, do what is being asked, and move on without a lot of complaining. They don't like it either, but they quickly cut through the bureaucracy driving the tasks in order to possess the time needed for what they want to enjoy. They look at their mindset more systematically than most. As you look to reinvent your mindset for the better, it is comforting to know two points of interest:

- Almost everyone must go through a mindset reset in order to redefine their experiences on the job.
- Every day provides you an opportunity to confront your habits of the mind and diagram them for the better.

The mind needs constant nurturing, reevaluating, and a sense of empathy expressed toward old lines of thinking. In his book *Creating Innovators: The Making of Young People Who Will Change the World*, Tony Wagner interviewed young innovators to discover their individual characteristics. He wanted to learn if there was a pattern or a commonality in the passion these individuals possessed that supported their *out of the box* mentalities. In his writing, he states the following about the students he interviewed:

I discovered a consistent link and developmental arc in their progression from play to passion to purpose. They played a great deal—but their play was frequently far less structured than most children's, and they had opportunities to explore, experiment, and discover through trial and error—to take risks and to fall down. Through this kind of more creative play as children, these young innovators discovered a passion. As they pursued their passions, their interests changed and took surprising turns. They developed new passions, which, over time, evolved into a deeper and more mature sense of purpose—a kind of shared adult play. (Wagner 2012)

When you look at the results from these discussions that Wagner had with young innovators, how can the findings be applied to today's educator in the schools? How do you accomplish new passions around what you have been doing every day in the schools? How do you develop a deeper sense of purpose like the student innovators described above?

The answers to these questions will not come in the form of restructuring a lesson plan, devising new assessment practices, or implementing the division's newly designed strategic plan for the masses. These are traditional ways of thinking, bureaucratic responses to a culture that prides itself on compliance to standard expectations. The actions have merit and provide guidance to the subordinates of the organization. However, the goals and objectives tend to recycle themselves over the years; rarely are you challenged to redevelop your sense of values around what you do and, in turn, discover a deeper passion.

As you look for that deeper sense of purpose and passion that will drive your innovation gene, look no further than the following excerpt from George Couros in reference to how educators can foster an innovator's mindset for their students. As you read these characteristics, you should adopt a lens of inquiry about yourself. In other words, how much of these attributes do you possess?

1. *Empathetic*—To create new and better ways of doing things, we need to first understand who we are creating them for. As educators, innovation starts with the question, "What is best for this child?" For us to create something better for our students, we have to understand their experiences and this is why it is imperative that we not only talk about new ways of learning, but immerse ourselves in these opportunities. This way we can understand what works and what does not work, from the perspective of a learner, not a teacher. If anything, teachers have to develop a deep understanding of learning before they can become effective in teaching. We need to put ourselves in our student's shoes before we can create better opportunities for them in our classrooms.

2. *Problem Finders*—As Ewan McIntosh talks about, it is important that we teach our kids how to ask good questions instead of simply asking for answers. All innovation starts from a question not an answer. The invention of the home computer started with the focus of, "How do we bring the experience of a powerful computer into the homes of families?" Many capstone projects developed by students in their classrooms start with first finding, and then solving problems, both locally and globally. How often do we, as educators, immerse ourselves in a similar process? If we want to be innovative, we need to look at questions first.

3. *Risk Takers*—Many would argue that "best-practice" is the enemy of innovation. To be truly innovative, you sometimes have to go off the beaten path. The reality of this is that, for some kids, the "tried-and-true" methods will still work, but others, you will need to try something different. In a time where many kids are totally checking out of school, is "best practice" truly "best" or just "most well-known"?

4. *Networked*—Steven Johnson has a powerful quote on the importance of networks where he states, "Chance favors the connected mind." Innovation does not happen in isolation, as it is often ideas that are being shared among many that lead to new and better ideas being developed. The best educators have always created networks to learn from others and create new and powerful ideas. Now though, many have taken the opportunity to take networks to a whole different level through the use of social media to share and develop new ideas. Isolation is the enemy of innovation. Networks are crucial if we are going to develop the "Innovator's Mindset."

5. *Observant*—A practice normal among those that would be considered "innovative" is that they constantly look around their world and create connections. It is normal to have a notebook or use their mobile device to record ideas or thoughts around them and link them to their own ideas. In education, we often look to solutions to come from "education," but when organizations around the world share their practices and ideas, we have to tap into their diverse expertise and learn from them as well. Wisdom is all around us; we just have to look for it.

6. *Creators*—So many people have great ideas, yet they never come to fruition. Innovation is a combination of ideas and hard work. Conversation is crucial to the process of innovation, but without action, ideas simply fade away and/or die. What you create with what you have learned is imperative in this process.

7. *Resilient*—Things do not always work on the first try, so what are the tweaks or revamping that is needed? To simply try something and give up as soon as it fails never leads to innovation, only a definitive end.

This is something great teachers model daily in their teaching, as they turn good ideas into great ones.

8. *Reflective*—What worked? What didn't? What could we do next time? If we started again, what would we do differently? What can we build upon? It is important that in education and innovation, we sit down and reflect on our process. This last point is definitely lacking in many aspects of education as we are always "trying to get through the curriculum," yet reflection is probably the most important part of education as the connections we make on our own is where deep learning happens.

By focusing on these innovative characteristics and breaking down what each one means for your own personal construct, you can begin to find the innovative areas that are most effective for your problem solving, planning, goal orientation, and overall disposition. In addition, you should be able to find

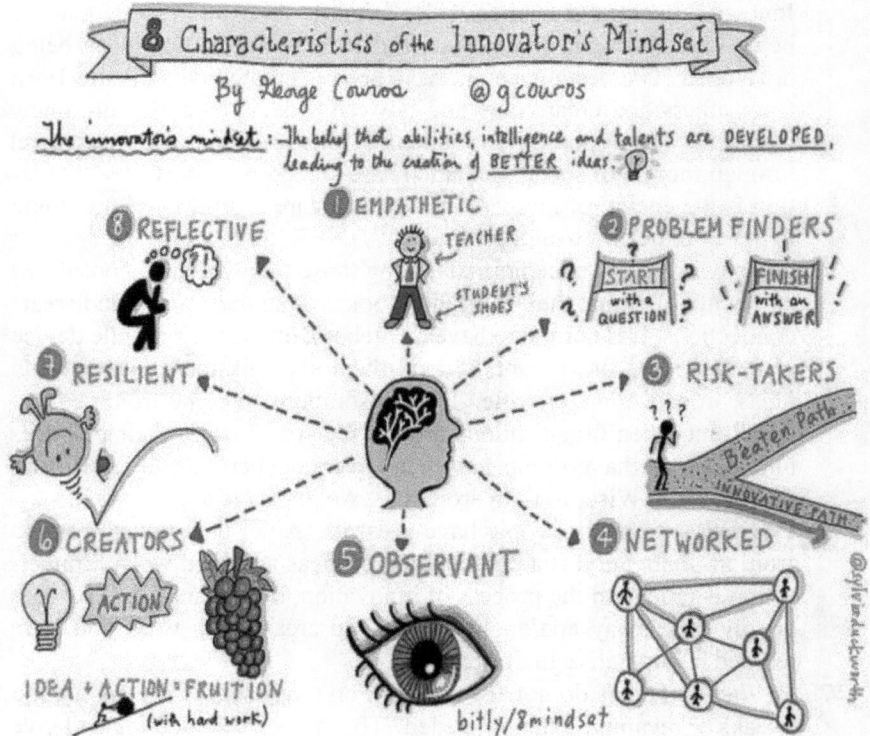

Figure 9.1.   Eight Characteristics of an Innovator's Mindset. George Couros

those innovative areas that need more work. By working toward encompassing all of these attributes as an educator, you will be best equipped to not just deal with today's technology-driven learner, but you will become more resilient and focused on keeping that main thing the main thing on a daily basis.

Solution Summary

- Innovator's Mindset: Empathetic, Problem Finders, Risk Takers, Networked, Observant, Creators, Resilient, and Reflective.
- Adopt a lens of inquiry about yourself.
- The highly focused and reflective educator's mind works to create opportunities every day where reflection is the norm, not the exception.
- Immediate action from a subordinate in reference to tasks issued = your boss oftentimes need not worry about you or your department.
- Individuals who fall into a play personality that is based on flexibility, imagination, and movement may find their mindset more flexible.

This chapter begs for the educator to conduct an intake on how innovative he or she is in the classroom and the school. As a teacher and school administrator, reviewing the characteristics of the innovator's mindset and asking yourself which categories possess a strength for you and which ones need to be addressed further is a big step in developing a more well-rounded mindset. It is also important to review these characteristics through various prisms in a school setting: How do these apply to you, as a teacher, in the classroom? How do these apply to how you plan lessons? How, as a school administrator, do these characteristics apply to disciplining a student or leading a faculty meeting?

Section III

Real World Application for the Solution-Focused Educator

Chapter Ten

Meetings at School

In this section of chapters, you will begin to learn how to apply the mindset strategies and mental tools that have been discussed in *real-world* settings. Strategies and solutions are only effective if you, as the reader, can learn how these suggestions and concepts can be applied to everyday life in the schools.

As meetings unfold and decisions are rendered in your classrooms and in your buildings, it is easy to stay in process or in collaboration mode. Everyone feels included and the belief that "something is getting done" presides. Unfortunately, permanent process can be a disease for staff culture. It creates the following philosophy: everybody is responsible so nobody is responsible. Meetings serve as constructive forums for information to be disseminated by teachers and administrators. Rules and procedures are often discussed. The information oftentimes is focused on policy reform, new initiatives and student interventions, and assessment practices.

Concerns arise when these forums become platforms for a verbal show and tell, on the part of some individuals, that does not concern the masses. Everyone's time becomes impacted by a few individuals. The personal needs of others should not override the allegiance to the fundamental purpose of the agenda itself. In order to constructively keep meetings (and online interactions) on task, leaders and coworkers must not perseverate on one problem (behavior or academic) unless two solutions are generated. Lengthy personal descriptions and backgrounds only serve as symbols of a compressed mindset attempting to disrupt the forum. Stimulants for derailment are then created and staff culture can suffer.

From a systems perspective, how can an organization/school ensure that they are not creating a labyrinth of complexity around agenda items that don't concern instructional practice? Logistically, the answer rests with the facilitator or the leader of the building to ensure that the meeting is about solutions. Time limits help. However, the leader of the meeting is often out of a teacher's locus of control. Unless you are the administrator, you may possess little control over who conducts the meeting and what topics will be the focus. If you are in this type of situation, the only focus you can control is the attitude you possess prior to, during, and after the meeting.

Deadlines that come out of meetings create the power of choice as well. Every day, all across the classrooms of many buildings, deadline-driven situations exist and beg for action. Individuals in schools that embrace deadlines and remove them quickly are the ones who have more time to dedicate to the responsibilities they most enjoy: working with students. Once a new initiative is funneled through the faculty, there seems to be two types of individuals:

- There are those who are bogged down by the existence of a new policy and yet another action request.
- There are those who already have devised an efficient manner in meeting this obligation and move forward.

CASE STUDY: CHRIS

Chris was a math teacher. He was a hardworking, soft-spoken individual who rarely wanted to participate in any other activities within the school. Chris often spoke about the challenges he faced with attending meetings that did not apply to his craft. Observing Chris in meetings and speaking with him afterward to learn how his emotional states fluctuated, the administrator learned a great deal about his frame of mind.

His comments led the administrator to believe that he seemed frustrated at the facilitator (in this case, the principal). Chris spoke about his thoughts to his administrator. Together, Chris and the administrator began to recognize that the meetings, at their surface existence, were what Chris defined as his source of discomfort. However, the discussions created a shift in his definition and reasoning. He began to think about how he was thinking more often (metacognition). He also took the time to diagram his stress and emotional reactions with meetings through the Hurricane-GIANTS concept.

Chris concluded that his internal conversations led to further stress. The voice in his head was complaining and judging and bemoaning the entire process (see figure 10.1). Moving forward, he made a more conscious effort to try the following:

- Monitor the internal voice that was complaining about a current situation.
- Work toward making it a habit.

- Become more introspective about himself and how he was handling the moment.

It wasn't a philosophical shift in Chris's mind as much as it was a *process* he began to develop. There wasn't any immediate transition to some type of positive mental attitude or simple shift in neurolinguistics. He still had issues with the content at faculty meetings. However, he learned how to apply the self-monitoring skills that worked for him and take more accountability for his attitude.

For teachers and administrators, oftentimes in professional meetings, it is not the content that is causing the emotional fluctuations. Rather, the conversation they are having with themselves is the compressed mentality that causes stress and frustration. The quality of your employment of language around your internal dialogue, on a second-by-second basis, is one of the most vital components to reframing your attitude. It requires an act of consistently monitoring the content of your thoughts. If you are judging and bemoaning the experience you are presently having in a parent conference or another meeting, you will continue to experience the senses of dissatisfaction, frustration, and irritability. These feelings will then set the table for the rest of your day in terms of how you experience and interpret life on the job.

MEETINGS TRIANGLE

Hurricane-GIANTS

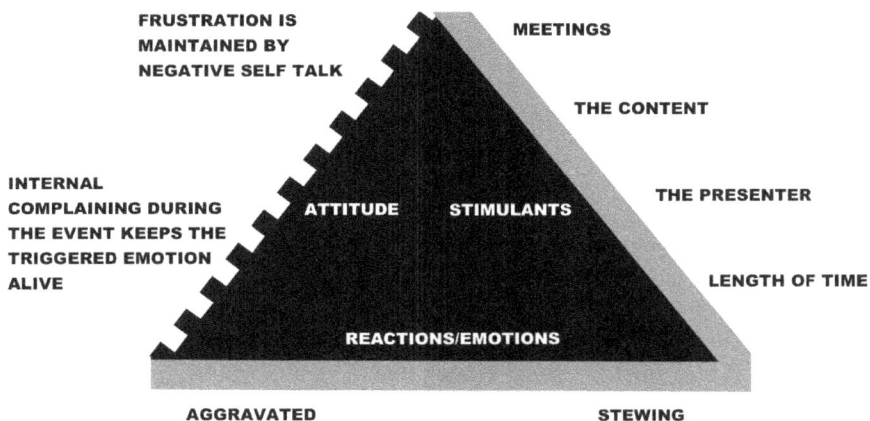

FRUSTRATION IS MAINTAINED BY NEGATIVE SELF TALK

MEETINGS

THE CONTENT

INTERNAL COMPLAINING DURING THE EVENT KEEPS THE TRIGGERED EMOTION ALIVE

ATTITUDE   STIMULANTS

THE PRESENTER

LENGTH OF TIME

REACTIONS/EMOTIONS

AGGRAVATED   STEWING

Figure 10.1.   Meetings Triangle. Graphic by Todd Franklin

CASE STUDY: MATT

Matt was a tenth-grade English teacher at a high school with class sizes that ran well over 30:1 ratios. The community was highly affluent and very involved with the school, possessing an active PTA that worked very hard to support the initiatives of the school for students and the teachers in the classrooms. Matt was in his ninth year of teaching and served as the department chair for his content area. He was a very strong teacher, and the students were well prepared for the eleventh grade by the end of the year. He was data driven and student focused and communicated a great deal with parents about the progress of each student.

One day, Matt approached his grade-level administrator to discuss how parent conferences were conducted at the school. Recently, over the past two years, Matt felt that the parents were blaming him and his colleagues for the challenges that their child was experiencing. Matt expressed that he felt defensive often in parent conferences and was beginning to feel resentful toward this important piece to a child's success: relationships with parents. As the assistant principal spoke to Matt about his feelings, it was quickly apparent that Matt was justified from the examples he shared. He talked about second chances, reassessing and notifying parents consistently about those students who were presenting challenges in the classroom.

After observing Matt and the cross-curriculum teachers in the parent conference setting, the administrator saw firsthand what Matt described. The teachers would outline their concerns and the parents would respond with the efforts they were making at home. Then, the conference would wrap itself up at the end with the teachers feeling they had addressed their concerns to the parents, but the parents found no solutions. In fact, the conferences ended with the parents asking, "What are you going to do now to help make sure my child is successful?" The team tried to talk about after-school assistance and retakes on assessments, but those had been interventions already applied without success. The bell would ring and the conference would conclude.

After a variety of observations, the administrator talked with Matt about how the conferences were structured. There were three suggestions that came out of the debrief:

1. Create an agenda or outline for the conference that is written for everyone to operate from on the same page.
2. The outline should be simple and direct: Areas of Strengths, Challenges Displayed, and Solutions/Action Items moving forward.
3. Pre-conference: By pre-conferencing with the teachers, some of the concerns could be summed up by one individual, leaving more time for *how to make sure the student is successful*.

After deploying these suggestions, Matt found his parent conferences were more focused on what he and the teachers could do moving forward instead of summarizing concerns and rehashing intervention strategies that were not working.

> How often do you check in with your thoughts? Are they driving your opinions and hijacking your emotions without you knowing it? Are you teaching on a continuum that symbolizes the status quo, or are you able to see clearly beyond the mandates and touch the soul of each child?

What causes this internal fixation on summarizing concerns without solutions? Prior school experiences, or life experiences for that matter, tend to govern your mentality in reference to how you approach certain issues. If previous experiences with parent conferences have been in conflict with your immediate perspectives at the time, a level of resentment may exist, like it did for Matt. These feelings then manifest themselves in a variety of situations moving forward. Stepping back and recognizing your preconceived perspectives about parent conferences or meetings in general is helpful. You may have the perfect justification for your feelings. A jury may even agree with you. However, being right and being content with situations around you are two very different categories of acceptance.

Solution Summary

- Individuals in schools that embrace deadlines and remove them quickly are the ones who have more time to dedicate to the responsibilities they most enjoy: working with students.
- Oftentimes stress is caused by the conversations you are having with yourself, ruminating about the issue as it continues to escalate in your mind.
- When running a parent conference: Have an agenda, pre-conference with one another to summarize concerns, and then leave time for the question: how are we going to make this student successful?
- Being right and being content with situations around you are two very different categories of acceptance.

In this chapter, you were asked to look at yourself in regard to how you think during the many meetings that are required of you as a teacher or administrator. The chapter introduced *food for thought* in regard to really focusing on how long you carry the internal complaining forward during and after the meeting. Again, you are introduced to the metacognition concept in this

chapter as a way to remind yourself to catch the thoughts before they intoxicate your feelings about the situation. Also, you learned about structuring
parent conferences with a solution-focused approach. Rather than having
each teacher summarize their concerns to the parents, consider electing one
spokesperson who can provide that feedback and then gain more time back
for generating a *what now* mentality.

Chapter Eleven

Grading and Reporting

Grading and reporting is always a consistent deadline and responsibility that all educators encounter every nine weeks. After all of the work of each quarter is complete, there is always a time when marks need to be issued to symbolize how each student is progressing in the classroom.

CASE STUDY: KELLY

Kelly was entering her nineteenth year in the school system when she came to the administrator's office at the end of the first quarter to discuss some final grades for a few of her students. She was the English department chair. In a very typical situation, she couldn't decide whether to give two particular students incomplete or failing marks for the quarter.

As she and the assistant principal dove further into their conversations, Kelly talked about the lack of effort on the students' part, the countless opportunities she had given them, and the misbehaviors that defined why these two students were in this position. They simply did not take advantage of the opportunities given to them to make up missing work, stay after school for help, and so on.

Kelly felt like there was a responsibility factor that these students did not exhibit and the failing mark was justifiable. As Kelly spoke, she seemed very agitated. She admitted to feeling very frustrated with these two students. Unfortunately, Kelly did not feel as if she was receiving the support from their parents in this situation as well. Kelly continued to discuss how hard she had worked and the countless hours spent trying to help these students, even though they had made her life extremely difficult in the classroom.

She felt like the e-mails she received from the parents were abrasive and unjustified. After listening to Kelly, the administrator asked her to put aside the movie. The administrator asked her to stop replaying or rereading the e-mails in her head and asked her to stop talking about the problematic situation. "Don't get pulled into a repetitive quandary on the same issues from one school year to the next," he expressed. Kelly was mystified at this response. It did not seem to help her at all.

Kelly and her administrator continued to discuss their individual philosophies around teaching and learning. "With too much process and discussion, you can struggle to meet the individual needs of specific situations," the administrator stated. Stepping outside of this example, one can see philosophical complications that can exist if conversations around grading and reporting are not a constant in the school. A variety of scenarios exist for why an incomplete mark is assigned. Incomplete marks are much like issuing zeros. The zero can misrepresent a student's overall performance. You don't want incomplete marks to create confusion at the end of a marking period. Kelly agreed she would attempt to stop fixating on the intangibles of the problems she could not control and focus more on whether the children could display mastery of the content.

After a few weeks of these discussions, Kelly made some valid attempts to remove the fixation of her problems with these two students. She reflected on her conversations with the administrator, thought about her mindset around this topic, and reached the following conclusion: "If I spend week after week and month after month discussing incomplete work, I lose focus on the moment." She was starting to realize the bigger picture and stopped allowing specific incidents that happened in the classroom to paralyze her emotional state. She refused to allow herself to be summoned back to a compressed mindset.

The Hurricane-GIANTS triangle assisted Kelly to focus more on her own attitude toward the circumstances being created for her by others (see figure 11.1). She was beginning to take the first steps to realizing the difference between an open and closed mentality. She was learning to digest a bigger picture in the classroom and not constantly looking for linear answers to problems that were circular in nature.

At times, incomplete marks may carry an ambiguous message. Though there is a need for incomplete marks to be assigned, the perception of ambiguity on the part of any student or parent can symbolize a communication breakdown. It creates conflicts and uncomfortable conferences. As Ken O'Connor stresses in his book *A Repair Kit for Grading*, one should not include zeros when determining grades when evidence is missing or incomplete. "Grades are broken when zeros are entered into a student's academic record for missing evidence or as punishment" (O'Connor 2007). Though there is not a perfect solution to "holding students accountable," you can take steps to influence your anxiety for the better. The following are four actions for incomplete marks:

- Use your best professional judgment in regard to rectifying incomplete marks. Though contacting the students and their parents is a requirement, your goal is to continue to identify mastery.
- Document with an e-mail or a phone call that the parents have been informed *and* you have received a response to those efforts.
- Invite parents into the equation. Avoiding communication with parents because you are preparing students for the real world is a challenge. Your landscape of comfort on the job will forever be challenged.
- Avoid telling yourself about how much needs to be done (that metacognitive practice strikes again!). Monitor how often you are restating time-sensitive thoughts to yourself. Then start to see if you can implement a different approach.

For Kelly, it helped for her to work on developing her sense of inquiry. In other words, she truly began to question her emotional reactions to experiences on the job every single day. It takes three weeks to build a habit, and this habit can reduce anxiety and improve your mood. For Kelly, in this situation, it worked. How do you promote this spirit of inquiry internally to change your actions externally?

This is the question that you should be asking yourself. Emotional change takes practice in a learning environment because schools are always chang-

GRADING TRIANGLE

Hurricane-GIANTS

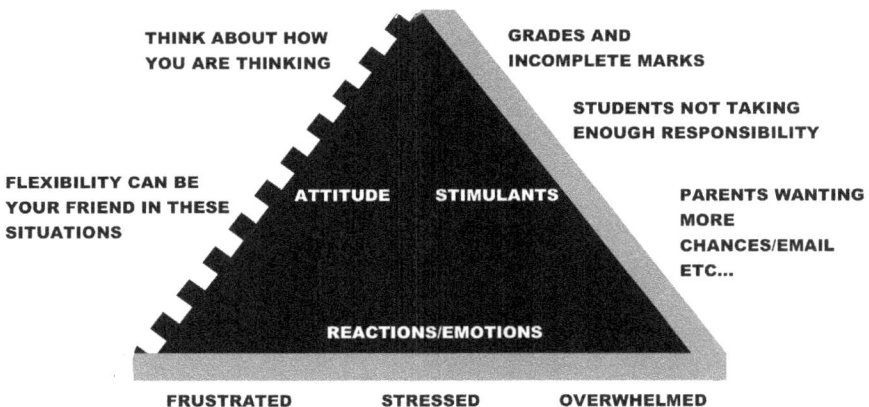

THINK ABOUT HOW
YOU ARE THINKING

GRADES AND
INCOMPLETE MARKS

STUDENTS NOT TAKING
ENOUGH RESPONSIBILITY

FLEXIBILITY CAN BE
YOUR FRIEND IN THESE
SITUATIONS

ATTITUDE   STIMULANTS

PARENTS WANTING
MORE
CHANCES/EMAIL
ETC...

REACTIONS/EMOTIONS

FRUSTRATED   STRESSED   OVERWHELMED

Figure 11.1.   Grading Triangle. Graphic by Todd Franklin

ing. If-then philosophies about predicting events are not always accurate. Linear individuals, especially in grading and reporting, want those predictions to be right because that creates a sense of emotional comfort. By establishing a habit of self-inquiry, you can redirect the focus of the perceived negative stimulant, in this case grading, and create solutions. Pacing guides, assessments, report cards, and e-mails are things. Things don't create energy; energy creates things. It starts with your ability to not ruminate about misbehaviors that make you lose focus on whether the child has mastered the content.

Highly successful educators who have mastery over their mindset learn to compartmentalize. They know when to navigate their responsibilities in a manner that minimizes the feeling of being overwhelmed. In her book *Lion Taming: The Courage to Deal with Difficult People Including Yourself* (1995), Betty Perkins discusses seeing difficult people as opportunities, not obstacles. Looking at challenging personalities or work ethic differences should be a catalyst for personal growth and not a stimulant for victimizing moments and yourself in the classroom.

In this example, Kelly could outline her triangle by listing the stimulants such as incomplete marks, students not taking responsibility, and lack of parent support. Her reaction line of the triangle (the bottom of the shape) would be characterized as frustrated, stressed, and overwhelmed. In order for Kelly to rebound and become more proactive around this problem, instead of being stuck in those typical reactionary measures driven by her emotions, she needs to keep fighting for how her attitude can be reshaped. It is the only option.

The only other option is to wallow in the frustration. Thus, her third leg of the triangle could be about flexibility and metacognition by using words/ phrases that can take her mindset to the following belief: this is common in everyday education. There will always be students who do not possess work habits for success, but is there enough evidence that exists for mastery of content to be displayed? This philosophy does not excuse the lack of work turned in, nor should it deflect from the grades the students earned. It is a mindset technique to bring Kelly and other teachers in these positions to a point where their mood is not so heavily impacted by cyclical, annual situations of the classroom.

Solution Summary

- Highly successful educators who have mastery over their mindset learn to compartmentalize.
- Looking at challenging personalities or work ethic differences should be a catalyst for personal growth and not a stimulant for victimizing moments and yourself in the school.

- As a teacher or administrator, you don't want incomplete marks to create confusion at the end of a marking period. Though there is a need for incomplete marks to be assigned, the perception of ambiguity on the part of any student or parent can symbolize a communication breakdown.
- Things don't create energy; energy creates things. It starts with your ability to not ruminate about misbehaviors that make you lose focus on whether the child has mastered the content.

In this chapter, as you consider your grading and reporting practices, the writing asks you to review your philosophies about incomplete marks both individually, as a teacher, and as a staff as a whole. What messages are you communicating with an incomplete mark? Creating a solution-focused mindset with incomplete marks starts with the end in mind.

Before issuing an incomplete mark, make sure you have a plan: What work needs to be turned in? How will it be assessed? How will you ensure the student has mastered the content? Be sure to ask yourself that last question over and over again. If you have a preponderance of evidence that indicates a student has mastered certain content areas, does the incomplete mark represent a lack of mastery or is it a logistical/work habit expectation of responsibility the student missed that truly is represented by the incomplete mark? These are the *nitty-gritty* specifics that need to be flushed out to move your mindset away from a fixed mentality and more toward a progressive, growth mindset.

Chapter Twelve

School Climate and Personalized Professional Development

Professional development (PD), just like social networking, is constantly changing and needs to be met, by school- and district-wide leaders, with a great sense of flexibility and exploration. Because of the online tools now readily available for PD, it is incumbent upon every educator in and outside of the classroom to view these opportunities through a lens of how to meet the immediate needs of employees today.

While participating in a three-day leadership seminar, a school-based administrator had the opportunity to work on a variety of self-reflective exercises with various district leaders in many capacities. They worked through an activity devoted to what makes a strong instructional program.

Aside from assessing test performance data, teacher input, and curriculum designs, many principals believed the overall focus should be on the academic, social, and emotional makeup of children. Successful instructional programs address the needs of individual students by measuring progress well beyond categorical academic assessments. Strong instructional programs also serve the essential life skills component for children by having a system in place that creates work habits for success. Most leaders of school buildings will assign teachers accordingly and increase instructional time as dictated by the master schedule.

CASE STUDY: TODD

Todd was a keynote speaker at the leadership conference and had led multiple school buildings at different levels. Todd spoke to one of the most underrated characteristics for a quality leader: the ability to de-escalate educational jargon into simple and concise steps of action. Todd knew how to embed this philosophy into the culture of the mind. He accomplished this feat by constantly providing forums for teachers that only had a two-fold focus: raising student achievement and raising a positive climate.

Raising a positive climate started with a focus on professional growth models where teachers constantly evaluated their instructional alignment through curriculum content validation matrices. When Todd would speak to his staff and would reference student performance on standards or specific benchmarking tools for achievement gap analysis, he knew, along with the staff, that standardized tests only represented a specific window of mastery for a student.

Analyzing gap data is a comprehensive task that needs to be viewed through the collaborative efforts of all the stakeholders of a school. How do teachers and administrators, with all that is on their plate, increase their collective tolerance for change and policy reform? Todd realized that the most effective leadership teams were the ones that offered PD specific to the skills of the teachers in the building. PD symposiums are usually the medium that delivers the change options and the policy deliverables for the following year.

- The best and most insightful PD sessions use one common thread: take current problems or responsibilities and show people how to solve them more efficiently.
- It's not about informing people. It's not about discussing strategies, creating information blogs, or showcasing online resources. It's about showing people their current challenges and then showing them how to solve them better.

Attention span is the amount of time one can spend on a given task without being distracted. Teachers and administrators must believe, in the first ten minutes, that the PD they are exposed to is worthwhile. Otherwise, by the eleventh minute, their professional minds and lives drive them back to the school or the stress of home life. Cautionary reticence should be exercised before pulling them out of their domains without valid, research-based practices that can give them something tangible to apply for the better. Generally, this required prism shift for teachers and administrators will not be accomplished solely through evaluation systems, required trainings, or influential colleagues.

The shift must be intrinsically motivated. Based on self-actualized, reflective exercises with their staff, leaders of schools can create conditions that manifest intrinsic motivation throughout the culture of a building. For example, the assessment process from one school to the next can be anxiety provoking on many levels. How will the formative and summative compo-

ASSESSMENT TRIANGLE

Hurricane-GIANTS

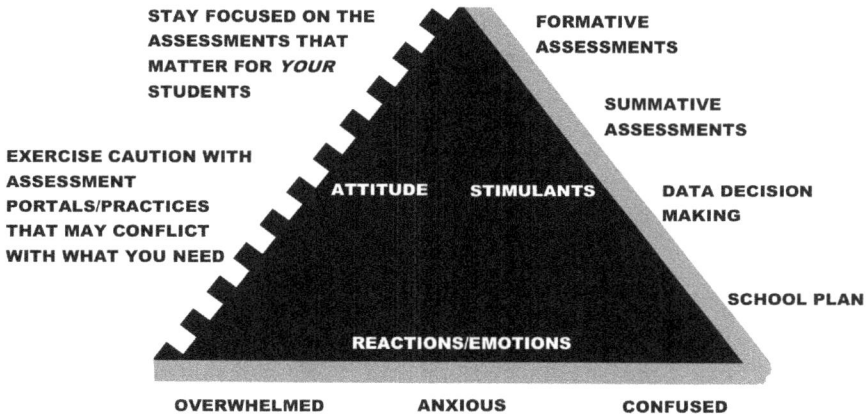

STAY FOCUSED ON THE
ASSESSMENTS THAT
MATTER FOR *YOUR*
STUDENTS

FORMATIVE
ASSESSMENTS

SUMMATIVE
ASSESSMENTS

EXERCISE CAUTION WITH
ASSESSMENT
PORTALS/PRACTICES
THAT MAY CONFLICT
WITH WHAT YOU NEED

ATTITUDE   STIMULANTS

DATA DECISION
MAKING

SCHOOL PLAN

REACTIONS/EMOTIONS

OVERWHELMED   ANXIOUS   CONFUSED

Figure 12.1.   Assessment Triangle. Graphic by Todd Franklin

nents look? What data will be analyzed? How will this be reflected in the school plan?

From figure 12.1, you can see how the staff can outline these concerns and focus more on their own individual thought and plan for problem solving. Once accomplished, only then can the layers of PD, in reference to the teaching craft and endless assessment practices, be authentically embraced. Successful PD that works begins with a needs assessment localized to the school. The development centers on analyzing the right data and considers intervention strategies specific to each student. Just as schools develop individualized success plans for students, it is fundamentally paramount for leaders to consider personalized PD that is job specific for the staff.

With this context as a preface, a school-based administrator should have a focused mindset on the following categories for the implementation aspects of requiring job-specific, personalized PD plans:

1. Ask employees to participate in a needs/skills self-assessment based on their professional experiences to outline possible skills or performance areas they would like to address further.

2. Analyze the results and begin with the goal definition process in regard to how the content/layout of the plans would appear in, for example, an online portal.
3. (Design phase) Collaboratively, develop an online personalized PD plan where adult learners (teachers) define the strategies they will deploy to meet goals (action steps and required support, how will it be measured?).
4. Implement a variety of training opportunities through a number of different mediums (flipped formats, webinars, face to face, how-to guides) to outline examples of goal strategies and evidence to display mastery of the skill and additional training symposiums around PD (i.e., PD focusing on one standard or key element within the job standard itself).
5. Conduct evaluations to determine the effectiveness of the personalized PD process, layout, trainings, and ease of use.

The above five steps require a mindset shift on the part of many. The central office and schools must work together to define how these individual PD platforms will look. After conducting and reviewing the needs/skills assessment results, it is critical for building leaders to make connections about those results. In turn, they can effectively develop goals in a collaborative manner in reference to what training would need to be considered. Reports that outline, for principals, the most common goals and objectives with their teachers will help discover the strategies and trainings they are anticipating to be most productive.

After reviewing the commonalties and assessing internal resources, a strict focus on timelines, deadlines, and communication methods for PD plans should take priority. As a leader, being progressive in your thinking and continuing to view how you can streamline your training to be personal and effective is critical. In the design portion of personalized PD, a leader needs to know how to bridge the expertise of the current teaching and learning teams with instructional technology personnel. Online PD transitional success is built on the effectiveness of this dyad. Building training modules require working with a variety of experts from many departments, tailoring efforts to the job specifications of employees.

For this particular action item, it is critical to discuss the term "job-specific" PD. From a visionary perspective, in reference to personalized PD, moving forward, the administrator's work should possess a precise focus on creating PD around the standards of the position (teacher, instructional assistant, support personnel). Linking PD with the evaluation process can be an online culture shift, allowing for educators to access content freely to meet their performance needs. Creating open mindsets around this type of PD can happen if school leaders are able to quickly display the advantages of the new formats (time savers, self-pacing).

When building these individualized plans around specific standards, however, leaders must understand how to *nurture and address the technology gap* within the profiles of their employees and meet them *"where they are"* in their training. Educators are faced with unprecedented opportunities to adapt a new mindset for PD that invites them to flip their understanding of training and support upside down with the advances in technology, social networking, and 24/7 accessibility.

The tiered intervention that is required is one that begins with accepting technology as a constructive asset and not an adversary. Essentially, co-teaching is not changing; *it has changed.* Technology is the second (or third) teacher in the classroom and is a very competent instructor with a variety of engagement tools. The classrooms that accept this notion are excelling at a rapid pace.

Classrooms need to be viewed as labs of experiences. Students are learning not just by doing but with the tools they utilize outside of school. Within a constant regressive spiral of philosophical shifts in technology, whereby management speaks to regulations and subordinates speak about what could be accessed and accomplished, mood fluctuations are to be expected. At this stage, with the rapid changes to how students are learning and processing information, educators are left to discover what works while building and implementing the newly adopted instructional and assessment frameworks. This causes a great deal of stress and anxiety for the individuals responsible for producing a learning environment that is conducive to today's learners.

Moods are impacted and fluctuate consistently based on the changes of the day. By providing lucid, online, and insightful strategies that are specific to the standards of performance (for building personnel, the central office, and support employees), PD can be intentional, personalizing content to meet the needs of educators. This would allow leaders to connect their PD efforts to the key elements within performance standards.

As an administrator, as you review the job specifications, it is paramount to continue your training focus on *how you will increase opportunities* for professional growth and development through the lens of your personalized PD plans. As per your school's job descriptions, you want to be sure to understand the *definitions and typical tasks* that are unique to each position and how to create a process that clearly outlines measurable steps for how each employee can meet the PD within those standards. *The more autonomy employees are given, statistically, the better performance that follows.*

By honoring this process, you can begin to capitalize on composing *online step-by-step* guides for personalized PD plans. In order to be effective with this composition, the training should be individualized and job-embedded. Leading a personalized PD cycle starts with allowing adult learners to learn at their own pace for their individualized training and gain information they need through a variety of online mediums, avoiding the labyrinth of complexity that can arise without the appropriate disposition around technology, change, and implementation.

In addition to the above steps, it is important to recognize the "buy-in" component to this process as it will relate to a change for employees. As with any PD initiative, understanding how to communicate the need, creating reasoning behind the inception of the change, and implementing a streamlined solution for all involved are important tasks. The messaging behind your efforts should be vetted from a number of different supervisory roles within the school district.

As a school-based leader, you want to generate conversations and plans around how you would ensure your leadership team members and administrators will be informed about the process and the avenues for support moving forward. As progressive as your flip training efforts may become, much of this information will be discussed by building leaders and leadership team members at the school level. With this reality in mind, it is important to establish clear and concise information up front with your central office in regard to the logistics of your transition efforts toward personalized PD.

The above steps symbolize the initial strategic plan you might introduce for implementation to ensure that you are taking constructive, research-based actions to meet your leadership responsibilities for personalized PD. As always, understanding the importance of learning from others, building relationships, and ensuring that the actions you take around any initiative would be based on collaboration and precedent are the keys to success.

Bridging the emotional divide between the employees who are technology savvy and comfortable with creating their own online plan and the novice users who may be *technology reserved* is to understand what it means to be a productive leader and effectively address the various mindsets that exist around PD. Effective school-based leaders, trainers, and support personnel know how to close the void that exists between the experiences many educators have on the job, as it relates to technology, and their reactive nature to them. From this perspective, recognizing preconditioned responses for creating PD plans online will be a culture shift for each employee. Teaching and supporting the learning *behind the whys* (and benefits) around this process of online job-specific portfolios will be a strong investment toward the success of its implementation.

Solution Summary

- The best and most insightful PD sessions use one common thread: take current problems or responsibilities and show people how to solve them more efficiently.

- Based on self-actualized, reflective exercises with their staff, leaders of schools can create conditions that manifest intrinsic motivation throughout the culture of a building.
- School-based administrators should have a focused mindset on the following categories for the implementation aspects of requiring job-specific, personalized PD plans: conduct a needs assessment, analyze results, design content around specific standards, develop online delivery system, evaluate the effectiveness.
- Nurture and address the technology gap.
- Technology is the second (or third) teacher in the classroom and is a very competent instructor with a variety of engagement tools.
- Classrooms need to be viewed as labs of experiences.

In this chapter, with a strong focus on PD, the writing asked school leaders to focus on how to deliver PD that is standard specific and online efficient. Aside from the above action plan that outlined the steps to a successful implementation of personalized PD, it is important not to overlook how this will be communicated to personnel.

A leader with an open mentality that embraces a growth mindset around PD understands the various learning platforms that need to be created for all individuals and continues to ask themselves what is it that teachers need now. Again, if classrooms are to be seen as project-based learning prisms, it must start with giving online opportunities for teachers to access content on their own time—self-directed. This type of autonomy builds trust and gives the teachers more time to plan for creativity as opposed to being removed from the classroom setting to attend another meeting.

Chapter Thirteen

Strategies for Conflict Resolution

Teacher-Teacher-Principal

Conflict resolution in the workplace is something that is always difficult and uncomfortable, especially between colleagues who need to work together every day. In this chapter, both as teachers and administrators, you will learn how to best resolve conflict so everyone can move forward in a manner that is best for students and the culture of the school.

One of the more difficult and unsettling decisions that many educators face in their careers is whether to move to another school. There is a myriad of reasons for why teachers or administrators choose a different school for employment. Based on the unpredictable, ever-changing circumstances in one's personal life, changing schools may be the solution. There are many, many good reasons for trying a different environment, and it is quite simply *not related to a closed mindset or thinking differently about a situation*. It is just time to leave.

As Susan Burkhauser states in her article, "How Much Do School Principals Matter When It Comes to Teacher Working Conditions?" 16 percent of U.S. public school teachers leave their schools each year. In her six-year study of North Carolina schools, Burkhauser found that teachers' perception of their schools' professional working conditions "greatly influences their decisions to leave their schools" (Burkhauser 2017). In her study, she divided professional working conditions into four areas and reviewed teacher feedback and responses accordingly: teacher time use, physical environment, teacher empowerment, school leadership, and professional development. After analyzing the results, she could clearly see that the key component to creating positive working conditions in schools *lies heavily on the principal*.

CASE STUDY: RICK

A twelfth-grade English team at a large high school was having many difficulties in understanding how the new pacing guide was going to be implemented in such a short period of time. They were also concerned about the
pacing from one quarter to the next. They received the new pacing guide in
May—five months before it was to be implemented. The team of teachers
asked to meet with the principal to discuss his expectations of them moving
forward. As Rick, the principal of the school, received these requests, he
believed that the inquires being raised by his English department were valid
but could wait until the summer. Rick was viewed by many as a very smart
and skilled instructional leader. He was a graduate of Harvard where he
earned his doctor of philosophy (PhD) in education.

As June approached, the teachers were becoming increasingly irritated at
Rick for not meeting with them and ironing out the specific expectations for
the next year in regard to this overhaul of their curriculum. In addition to the
pacing guide change, the two leaders of the team were in conflict over how to
plan for the change. The conversations had become intense between the two
teachers, and it was beginning to spread through the culture of the school.

The instructional concerns centered on how they would create a curriculum validation matrix that would outline the essential benchmarks and material that needed to be taught but more importantly the skills needed for the
students. The relationship concern was how these two teachers were going to
coexist moving forward after all of the in-fighting that was taking place
during the last half of the school year.

As it was June, much of Rick's time was spent on graduation preparation,
the students not graduating, disciplinary hearings, and the concerns of the
parent community. Because all of this schedule crashing happens in June
each year, Rick was hard-pressed to shift gears and focus on the plans for
next year and solve the relational issues within the team. So how did Rick
and the teachers get to this point? What could be looked at differently?

There is no easy answer to this dilemma. Teachers want answers and
guidance from leadership about next year. Leadership is trying to keep the
boat afloat *for today* in order to meet the immediate needs of students, parents, and other teachers *this year*. In order to learn more about the leadership
climate in all schools, the school district issued a climate survey. The climate
survey was distributed at a very, very busy time of the school year: May and
June. These tend to be the months where staff culture is at its lowest due to
the stress of end-of-year exams, graduation activities, parties, transitional
planning, and grading procedures.

Each year Rick reviewed the categories of the survey. He noted his teachers did not feel heard or understood. Rick was working hard and doing his
best and thought he was supporting his teachers. So, if the success of a

positive school climate is related to the effectiveness of a principal, and he has received high marks on his own evaluation, where is Rick to turn?

For someone like Rick, it is not about his intellectual quotient that is inhibiting his effectiveness. Rather, it is Rick's inability to see the bigger picture around the emotional validation that his subordinates need in order to feel heard and understood (emotional intelligence quotient). It wasn't that Rick displayed a conceited, all-knowing attitude. In fact, his disposition was the complete opposite: easygoing and humorous. What Rick failed to see was the importance of the relational component between what the teachers deemed important and what Rick believed to be a priority. His failure was not in effort. His failure was his inability to sense when to take the time for others. He needed to learn how to recognize and honor these needs from the teachers habitually.

Rick worked with his boss on the climate survey results. Much of what they discussed was centered on how to reframe his approach to the staff when they are asking for his guidance. Using the Hurricane-GIANTS method of emotional diagramming, Rick can define the stimulant (first leg of the triangle) as teacher requests and the emotional reaction on his part (second leg) as feeling overwhelmed and frustrated. The final leg of the triangle (negotiable attitude toward emotions) is the intervention he must practice. Rick must recognize that his emotional state and habitual interpretation to the stimulant (teacher requests) need to be altered. If he can create that "stop gap," before ignoring the requests, Rick can improve.

As an administrator, trying to rescue the strained relationships within a group of teachers is a challenge. By focusing on the concerns that define the problem and considering the surrounding elements that may be contributing to the issue, the rescue attempts can be successful. A sensitive understanding of people and their symbolic relationship with organizations is critical. Many change efforts fail not because the school-based administrator's intentions are incorrect or insincere, but because they are unable to handle the interpersonal dynamics within the problem itself.

In his publication *Teaching Smart People How to Learn*, Chris Argyris states that employees inevitably respond to frustrations by withdrawing psychologically, becoming indifferent, passive, and apathetic. They focus on identifying and correcting errors in the external environment. Solving problems is important. Argyris continues by calling for a need to reflect critically on your own behaviors, identify the ways they often inadvertently contribute to the organization's problems, and then change how you act.

Indeed, these characteristics were becoming part of how the English department was reacting to Rick. He was beginning to feel a sense of resistance from the teachers as he tried to engage them at the very end of the year. Rick was in need of reframing how he problem solved and had to become more reflective in order to make the progress needed. In his book, Argyris states the following:

> Highly skilled professionals are frequently very good at single-loop learning. After all, they have spent much of their lives acquiring academic credentials, mastering one or a number of intellectual disciplines, and applying those disciplines to solve real-world problems. But ironically, this very fact helps explain why professionals are often so bad at double-loop learning. Put simply, because many professionals are almost always successful at what they do, they rarely experience failure. And because they have rarely failed, they have never learned how to learn from failure.
>
> So, whenever their single-loop learning strategies go wrong, they become defensive, screen out criticism, and put the "blame" on anyone and everyone but themselves. In short, their ability to learn shuts down precisely at the moment they need it the most. The propensity among professionals to behave defensively helps shed light on the second mistake that companies make about learning. The common assumption is that getting people to learn is largely a matter of motivation. When people have the right attitudes and commitment, learning automatically follows.
>
> So, companies focus on creating new organizational structures—compensation programs, performance reviews, corporate cultures, and the like—that are designed to create motivated and committed employees. But effective double-loop learning is not simply a function of how people feel. It is a reflection of how they think—that is, the cognitive rules or reasoning they use to design and implement their actions. Think of these rules as a kind of "master program" stored in the brain, governing all behavior. Defensive reasoning can block learning even when the individual commitment is high, just as a computer program with hidden bugs can produce results exactly the opposite of what its designers had planned. Companies can learn how to resolve the learning dilemma. What it takes is to make the ways managers and employees reason about their behavior a focus of organizational learning and continuous improvement programs. Teaching people how to reason about their behavior in new and more effective ways breaks down the defenses that block learning. (Argyris 1991)

After talking with his superintendent, Rick worked to find ways to invest in these particular individuals by focusing more on this double-looping concept: how he was thinking and reasoning. Rick started to listen more than talk. In order to accomplish this task for Rick and other leaders in his position, open dialogues with the teachers needed to take place. There needed to be a forum where their attitudes toward the new pacing guide could be shared without judgment. With more directives and tighter controls, the teachers felt their autonomy had been taken away.

By participating in open dialogues with Rick, the teachers felt an uptick in their morale and productivity for the pacing guide component to their problem. By facilitating more of these discussions, some of the teachers' assumptions or beliefs could be uncovered and more progressive mindsets could be created. In regard to the relationship issue that existed with the two teachers, Rick chose to have the teachers speak together with him in his office. He then allowed them to speak with one another in the office without his influence or presence. The teachers were able to resolve some of their issues.

Analyzing the social and personal needs of individuals in a workplace is the key ingredient to improving work performance and morale. Taking into account the human dynamics of this issue and creating a platform of communication in the building that symbolizes joint decision making and horizontal leadership leads to effectively influencing the mindsets of individuals so they are more receptive to change. In reviewing strategies for teacher-to-teacher and principal-to-teacher conflicts, it is imperative to understand the importance of nurturing a contentious dyadic relationship in the workplace. There are many opportunities, in any organization, to have conflicting perspectives between personnel, both colleague to colleague and superior to subordinate. Though these two relationships differ in context, the solution steps to resolving these conflicts are quite similar.

Teacher to Teacher

- Understand that in any conflict between two people, both parties need to be heard, individually, without interruption. By providing a platform for each teacher to state their complaint, justify their position, and express their present feelings about the relationship, the administrator/mediator is able to honor the perspectives of both parties. Without this platform, each party is thinking about their own rebuttal, failing to truly hear one another.
- The administrator, after letting both parties express themselves, needs to shift the focus of the existing conflict back to the bottom line: *We are here for the students*. Though an obvious statement, the conflicts that arise between colleagues are mostly due to (a) personality conflicts or (b) equity in responsibility. Neither of these common stimulants for conflict involves students directly. However, reframing the teachers' personal constructs toward one another can be futile if they do not exercise flexibility. Thus, the focus needs to shift to the job, the students, and what they are charged with every day.
- As a final solution step, the mediator (administrator) should set a tone for the individuals to talk between one another by themselves, without oversight from their superiors. At the surface, this may seem risky. However, if the right ground rules are discussed, the teachers can realize their disagreements are often fixable. At the very least, a platform of *"agree to disagree"* can be helpful. This can increase the percentage chance of solvability and a pathway forward by simply getting to that point and releasing resentment.

Principal-Teacher

In a conflict that is based on a principal-teacher disagreement(s), the steps are similar: (a) both parties express themselves, (b) the principal sets a tone of respect and professionalism, and (c) a solution-focused mentality is implemented with take-aways. Obviously, the difference, in this dyadic conflict, is that the responsibility lies solely in the hands of the principal to resolve the issue with a subordinate.

- As the supervising authority in the building, the principal must discover how to navigate the conflict and the relationship in a manner that provides the teacher with the best learning environment moving forward. No matter the disagreement, that teacher is returning to the classroom to teach and support children. The principal must keep this fact in mind and carefully express themselves in a manner that respects the feelings of the teacher.
- Within the communication episode between the principal and the teacher, the principal must be skilled at moving the conversation in a direction that honors the work of the teacher while summarizing their differences in a respectful manner. The principal may disagree with the teacher's perspectives, but there must be an acknowledgment of feelings for the relationship to truly move forward.
- Though the principal-teacher conflict suggestions tend to appear like the administrator burdens the responsibility (even if a teacher is in the wrong), the reality is that the principal needs to ensure the teacher feels heard, understood, and supported. One can always rely on documentation, but, in reality, it is best to listen, process, and communicate a message of working together and keeping lines of communication open, not write in an e-mail or start an immediate move to formal documentation.

Solution Summary

- Analyzing the social and personal needs of individuals in a workplace is the key ingredient to improving work performance and morale.
- In a conflict, by providing a platform for each teacher to state their complaint, justify their position, and express their present feelings about the relationship, the administrator/mediator is able to honor the perspectives of both parties.
- Depending on the situation, the mediator (administrator) should set a tone for the individuals to talk between one another by themselves, without oversight from their superiors.
- Try to avoid e-mailing disagreeable opinions to colleagues and parents. This tends to escalate issues and cause rifts between parties.

In this chapter, much of the focus was centered on conflict resolution techniques between teachers or between teachers and the administration. One of the very fundamental keys to the success of resolving conflict is to speak in person. Technology tools, because of social networking, have revamped how people communicate and relate to one another.

Online habits, at times, are difficult to keep on the back burner when the communication of choice is text, e-mail, or posting. However, conflict resolution is difficult to process and move forward if there is not a live discussion between parties. Part of displaying a growth mindset that is open to change is to be able to engage in communication episodes where opinions may differ but the end goal is to solve, grow from the experience, and move forward. Argyris addressed the double-looping idea as reflection for how people think, the cognitive rules or reasoning they use to guide their actions. This type of understanding is only going to be discovered through personal, face-to-face communication, in turn increasing the possibility of the issues being resolved within the dyad that is having difficulty.

Personal Growth for the Solution-Focused Educator

Chapter Fourteen

Social Networking, Learned Shifting

Millennials and Beyond

Social networking and the variety of technology tools at the educator's disposal are growing at a rapid pace. Today's learners are begging for more autonomy *through learning by doing* and exploring the myriad of tech tools to help them research, decipher information, and learn on a different teaching continuum from the past. As constructive as these tools can be for the teaching and learning prism in today's classrooms, there is also an undercurrent of concerns that may arise with their application.

CASE STUDY: BRIDGET

At one particular conference, Jack, a principal, was discussing the challenges of texting, Twitter, e-mail, posting, and social networking (in general) with teachers, students, and parents. Over the past ten years, the landscape of teaching and learning in the classroom has rapidly changed.

In this discussion, Jack began to talk to the audience of teachers and administrators about a young teacher he had on his staff named Bridget. Jack described her as someone who was fresh out of college and seemed to be on the cutting edge of *technology in education*, always seeking new ideas to teach children. She was well versed in the social networking world of her students as well. Her résumé and references all spoke to a highly qualified individual who was anxious to start her career. After another round of interviews, Jack hired Bridget as his new journalism instructor.

During the first semester, Bridget bonded well with the staff and the students. The children seemed to appreciate her demeanor, personality, and sense of "fairness." The parents were happy with her communication and believed she was a wonderful addition to the school. As the spring semester approached, Bridget conducted a blog and wiki activity with her students.

This social networking project unfortunately became an opportunity for students to engage in some inappropriate discussions. As can be natural, Bridget began to fall into the online communication trap of expressing her personal beliefs and reactions to student's comments. The flipped classroom was more focused on the latest drama from various nightly postings than the assigned educational task. Though Bridget certainly maintained her professionalism and met her instructional obligations during the day, she found herself commenting about social problems the students were experiencing at night. In turn, the students inevitably viewed Bridget as a friend.

The students maintained personal blogs and were active members online in regard to instructional contributions. They were always excited about Bridget's class. Bridget was careful not to expose her personal blog to the children, but of course the blog was discovered. After many months of working through the trials and tribulations this caused Bridget, she and Jack sat down to discuss her mindset for creating a blog and why it had become such a staple to her existence.

Bridget talked, in great detail, about the need to document her life with pictures and captions. "It started out as a creative and fun way to keep track of my life," she explained. She discussed how blogging and Facebook postings seemed like the perfect place to store memories. It was something she had been doing since she was much younger. Then Bridget began to talk about the addiction she had to posting her pictures and opinions online and scrolling through Facebook for hours. It became an identity. She had essentially created an *online life* that was vastly different from her normal day-to-day existence in the classroom.

The postings became much more than just pictures and captions. She began to express opinions and reactions to situations in her life and others. She spoke about a sort of "rush" she received from reading the advice and opinions from people she had never met. It soon became this cathartic forum for her to escape to at the end of the day. Facebook and the like became the first act of communication in the mornings. Before she raised herself out of bed, Bridget buried her attention into the screen to check the social life of others and how many people *liked* her posted pictures and comments. She couldn't hit the refresh button fast enough. It had become an addiction.

This blogging/posting/commenting habit of communication creates a unique teaching and learning prism. Many students and teachers use this medium to discuss topics, advertise their perspectives, and disclose opinions. Social networking practices serve as an outlet to document lives, challenges, achievements, and so on. In some cases, however, blogging and posting can subconsciously illuminate personal issues. Confidentiality suffers. There is much to be gained from documenting your life for reflective purposes. Posting pictures and sharing them with others sustains relationships that are geographically challenging. However, when it begins to serve as an emotional crutch that interferes with a teacher's ability to educate children, it becomes a problem.

According to Jack, Bridget felt like the responses she received from her online followers served as an independent attestation for her written perspectives. Jack began to realize that Bridget's allegiance to this online forum created personal challenges. As Jack researched more about this topic, he sought out an expert on social networking and the beliefs behind the online activist. He began to learn that:

- Online activists may cloak bloggers or social network postings in a mantle of wisdom.
- The opinions and thoughts from others, even strangers, can actually, at times, override the perspectives of colleagues and family members.
- The anonymity of the blogger serves as an unbiased, nonconfronting source that people may view as safe and more credible. Thus, in theory,

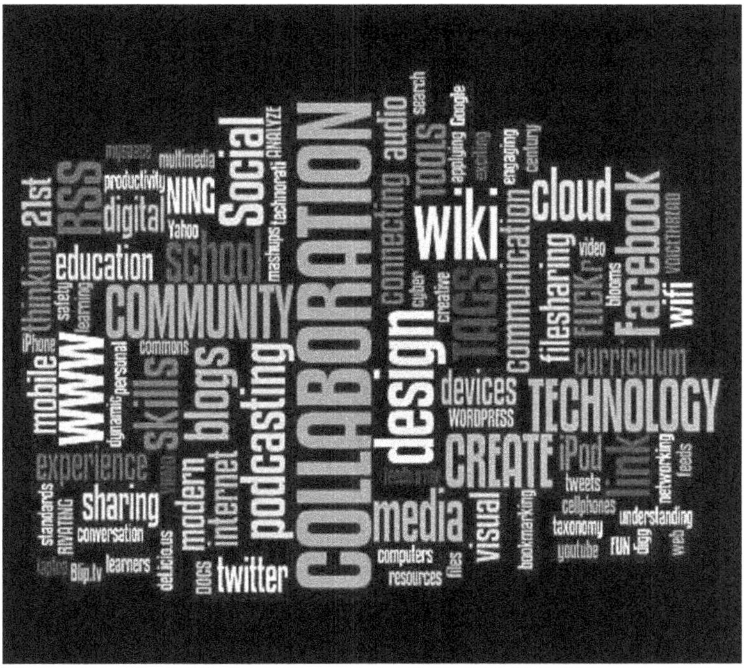

Figure 14.1.   From Google Images

the blogger may actually put a complete stranger's opinion beyond re-proach, a paragon of virtue if you will. If not handled with care, social networking can triangulate real issues, inhibit your problem-solving abil-ities, and create a utopian world that survives on status updates, likes, and postings.

As Jack stressed to Bridget, "Do not rob yourself from the most important teacher you will encounter—your mind—by adhering to the voices and opin-ions of others."

- Monitor your social networking accessibility and usage.
- As an educator of children, advertising personal thoughts, feelings, and perspectives can be a recipe for challenges in and outside of the class-room.
- Discover a more private approach to problem solving/journaling and de-velop a more sophisticated understanding of how to constantly explore and manage online educational forums.

Bridget stopped seeing Jack as being stuck in the past and more as someone who could help her adopt a more conservative approach to her teaching craft, minimizing online forums. The inner turmoil Bridget had experienced over the previous twelve months dissipated because of the support and advice Jack offered.

Using the triangle concept in this type of situation allows someone like Bridget to outline her experiences (stimulants) and her reactions/feelings to how she felt when the blog was discovered and then reframe her approach. The first line of the triangle would be stimulants such as posting, responding, communicating, and opinions. The second line of the triangle would be em-barrassed, uneasy, exposed, and frustrated. Finally, with these two states of mind linked together, it was on Bridget to outline how her attitude toward this problem was going to change. The answers on her mental triangle might be limiting her online habits, only discussing the educational task at hand, and removing students who were not able to keep the conversations profes-sional.

CASE STUDY: JANET

The responsibilities for teachers and administrators can be divided into three components: instructional practice/hiring, managerial responsibilities, and learned shifting. Because some educators can sometimes remain in their own educational silos, the action of learned shifting for the individual teacher or

The Social Networking Triangle

Hurricane-GIANTS

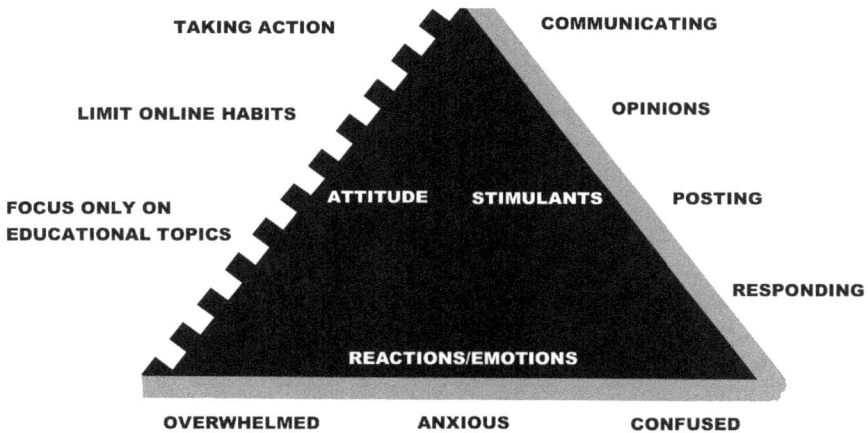

TAKING ACTION

COMMUNICATING

LIMIT ONLINE HABITS

OPINIONS

FOCUS ONLY ON
EDUCATIONAL TOPICS

ATTITUDE   STIMULANTS

POSTING

RESPONDING

REACTIONS/EMOTIONS

OVERWHELMED   ANXIOUS   CONFUSED

Figure 14.2.   The Social Networking Triangle. Graphic by Todd Franklin

administrator is difficult to master. What is learned shifting? What does this jargon actually mean for classroom teachers and leaders of buildings?

Janet was a middle school English teacher. She was a career switcher and was driven by the idea of teaching children. It was a passion of Janet's ever since she was a little girl. In her third year, it became apparent to the administration that Janet had a lot of instructional talent. However, she had a need to *control how* her students learned. She struggled with the *changing ways* in which children were learning in the twenty-first century.

As change happens in the culture of schools, understanding how students and teachers relate to one another on a daily basis is paramount. With teaching and learning becoming enmeshed in the social networking frenzy, there is a structural problem that exists if teachers and administrators do not feel a fundamental sense of urgency to change how students will learn in their classrooms. Because technology in the classroom is here to stay in a variety of formats, flexibility and less rigidity in the learning cycle should be an expectation for the mindsets of all educators.

Janet wanted to gatekeep every assignment the students would produce through certain websites and online platforms. Of course, monitoring and setting ground rules for which sites would be appropriate was essential. However, Janet did not want to accept any further responsibilities that may ask her to gatekeep any other idea(s) the students presented in the forums that may be inappropriate.

Today's teachers and school-based administrators are faced with unprecedented opportunities to adapt to a profession that begs to flip the teaching and learning cycle upside down with the advances in technology. As leaders in the classrooms and leaders of a school building, with the wave of technology initiatives that have captured the twenty-first-century learner, there has been a sort of cautionary reticence around how to implement these *bring your own devices to school* initiatives. This reticence has served schools well; however, it can also be a stop gap for adopting change in classrooms. Learned shifting in schools is the act of becoming more comfortable with the following *moving forward* statements:

- Moving forward, children will communicate more in writing than the spoken word.
- Moving forward, children will consistently expose their deepest thoughts, feelings, perspectives, and pictures to the world.
- Moving forward, children will beg for exhibitions of instructional mastery through the use of technology, of which they will most likely know more about than the adults in the building.

Children today are far less concerned about their digital footprint than in years past. Obviously, this creates concerns for parents, teachers, and administrators. Because children are processing information at such a rapid pace, the immediate concern for consequences, at times, takes a back seat for students. Students are going to make online mistakes. They are going to be exposed to age-inappropriate material. This understanding, however, should not inhibit educators from utilizing these online instructional tools for learning. The reservoir of trust in yourself can become shallow if you are not willing to try, change, and adapt to the tablet generation of learners that are thirsty for exploration and creativity from the learning environment.

As the assistant principal spoke with Janet, he reinforced some of his own beliefs around children and consequences in terms of ideological shifts in education. He talked about how he had seen the community, the families, the kids, the teachers, and the culture of education change over three decades. He observed the changes from the same classroom through the same prism. He observed the changes through the eras of cable television, Walkmans, cell phones, the Internet, social networking sites, tablets, and so on. So much had evolved technologically and yet so much had come undone, he uttered.

He continued in his discussion with Janet: kids are kids and will always be kids. Communities change and gadgets are created, but it is the bedrock of consequences that has shifted. Shifts in technology, shifts in what society values, shifts in school-wide expectations, and shifts in social influences are shifts that will always exist. The shift that has changed kids today is the fear of consequences that once governed how they shift.

As he told Janet, one of the most challenging concerns facing parents today is social networking accessibility for children. Unfortunately, many children set up their parents' online profiles or have access to their social networking habits, posts, and texts. The most detrimental part of this issue is not so much the material children may be exposed to on any given day. The millennial generation, because of their access to their parents' social networking sites/apps, possesses blurred lines between what was once a strict hierarchical relationship between the parent and the child.

Today's children hear their parents discuss rules and behavior; however, they are reading and viewing all of the adults' thoughts, feelings, problems, and postings in the neighborhood. This presents a sense of hypocrisy for the child. He or she begins to see adults as equals over time. Their underdeveloped frontal lobes are not mature enough to draw the distinction needed to view consequences as a deterrent when they are subconsciously considering the source. The conversation itself served as a reminder for Janet in regard to how and why today's children, at times, may be viewing authoritative figures, moving forward, as peers.

Janet did not want to accept the rapidly changing world of learning and producing through social networking, blogging, and posting. The assistant principal discussed this technology issue at length with Janet. He talked about his belief that, without accepting this concept of learned shifting and inviting its presence in classrooms, Janet (and other like-minded educators) would contribute a disservice to the craft that they work so tirelessly to master. Who Janet is as a teacher today *should be* completely different ten years from now if she wants to grow as a professional. The administrator felt it was important for Janet to understand this as a fact and not a random interpretation by the assistant principal.

In order to break through Janet's compressed mindset, the administrator met Janet where she was, in her current line of reasoning. He asked Janet to self-reflect at a much deeper level. The administrator worked on two specific points with Janet:

- Learn how to reason and develop a coherent argument with herself that justified why she *would not adopt* this concept of learned shifting and change in general. The administrator wanted Janet to brainstorm all the reasoning around *why she did not* think technology was needed in her classroom. He asked her to speak to *all* the ideas that contradict the reasons for change.

- Through these introspective conversations, the administrator was able to transition Janet—but not through mandates or technology-driven philosophies. He was able to bring her to a point of discovery. Janet began to think about *how to dissect her own engrained habits* of problem solving. This allowed her that bridge of transition (or awakening) for seeking another teaching method and getting students to think differently.

This idea of learned shifting was intimidating to Janet. It challenged her teaching philosophy to the core. The conversations she was having with her administrator broke through the instructional alliance she had with herself in regard to what she *always believed* was best for children. Janet had to learn to accept that students may actually know more about how to use the technology tools and resources for learning than she did.

Eventually, after Janet and her administrator exhausted all the arguments and justifications *for not changing the way* Janet taught students, project-based learning and the buffet of online teaching tools became more of a staple in her classroom. Socratic online seminars allowed for Janet to see the benefits of kids learning at home, in a flipped classroom, while keeping them engaged with technology.

By observing her peers and learning from the folks she already knew, Janet was able to see the value of something new and embrace those changing beliefs into her instructional practice. She became more versed with understanding that her emotional reactions are linked to situations where it is her choice to decide how the events of the day will impact her moods.

After a few months of changing how her students learned in the classroom, Janet and the administrator continued their conversations around change and the teaching and learning cycle. They discussed the term *producing regardless*. Often times, this "producing regardless" terminology refers to achieving a specific level of performance on the job no matter what circumstances exist. For their purposes, Janet and her supervisor used this term as an accountability measure for how Janet was going to continue to bake various opportunities of student choice into her lessons.

Getting her mindset ready, initially, to tackle new initiatives was a challenge. The key for Janet was to first recognize her inhibiting thought patterns to change and then know what action to *take against* her old line of teaching. Her goal was to produce an energy level and a focus that challenged her first instinct. Tony Robbins, a well-known motivational speaker, talks about how the most important thing in your life is the mastery of your state. He stresses the importance of recognizing the relationship between peak states and your specific thoughts and verbal expressions about subjects. He notes, after a period of time, people begin to associate and adopt states of mind with topics/things they are consistently focusing on throughout a given period (Robbins 1992).

The Thread

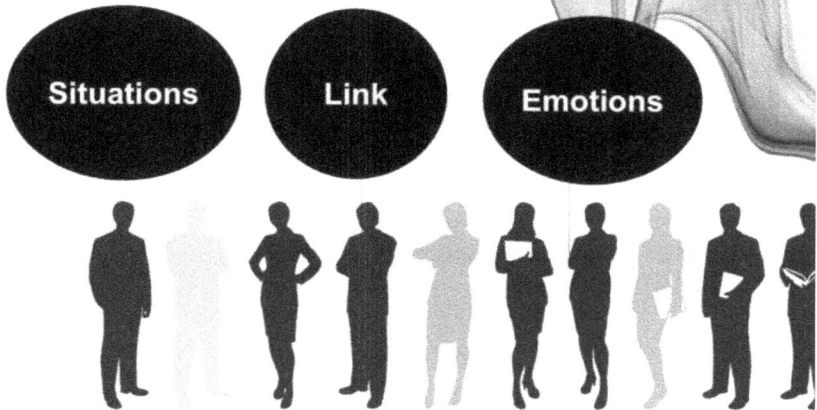

Figure 14.3. The Thread Graphic produced using Keynote template by Todd Franklin

For Janet, this was the answer. The more she could focus on changing her instinctive methods, the more confident she became. It wasn't about immediately changing what she did in the classroom. It was about her self-discovery, after debating all the reasons not to change, which allowed her to *be willing* to tackle something new. In the school, your states of mind, if not monitored, can fluctuate and respond to a variety of unpredictable episodes. Your emotional states and reactions to these problems are what you need to anticipate before they invite themselves back to your old way of thinking.

For teachers like Janet, the solution to overcoming these regressive instructional spirals resides in the teacher's ability to develop an attitude that is, ironically, more receptive to unpredictability. Embracing this as a fact, as opposed to resisting its existence, is the key. As Janet learned, the solution framework to flipping her attitude and closing parts of her personal achievement gap started with recognizing *the habitual* "what if" style of thinking. She began to count how many times she was predicting the future negative events four or five steps ahead of the actual experience.

For Janet, she found great success in achieving more peak states of mind by counting, during the day, each time she caught her thoughts jumping on the judging and predicting train. A strong first step in achieving this practice consistently, for Janet, was to bridge her IQ and her emotional intelligence to an engaged level, questioning her own status quo and viewing the LEARN model differently.

For school-based administrators, this "producing regardless" mentality starts with reviewing your own leadership of values, which has governed how and why you make decisions. As a principal, looking at how you connect people around what they are passionate about and what drives them provides a more seamless road for change. As a principal, you want to get teachers excited about their changing craft. Connecting teachers to learning about what drives them is the engine to success.

As a leader, you must avoid, as best you can, becoming bogged down by red tape that you cannot control. Working to get people to reframe their thinking about what it is to participate in the education of students starts with getting them to reflect on their own professional construct. Work with teachers to better understand the importance of matching what they value on the job to the action plan to get there more often.

Value Proposition Discussions

As a leader of an organization, value proposition discussions are critical to bringing teachers to this next level of producing regardless around the twenty-first-century learner. Challenging *the why* behind what teachers currently state is the *value for why they choose to teach a certain way* is the conversational starter. Oftentimes, in any organization, people can lose sight of their sense of purpose because of the ever-changing demands of the job.

Leaders should always try to see the subordinates of the organization as people first. Once this belief and perception are created, getting teachers at the strategy table for their own self-improvement becomes an increased possibility. As a leader, if you want teachers to set new learning goals, think differently about their current practice, and truly consider change, then see them as people first through personal reflection exercises. Subordinates, in any organization, must see that you care about them as people. This process allows teachers to begin to see multiple values in their focused efforts. If school-based administrators create and model habits that focus on a deeper understanding of the emotional intelligence quotient, other doors will open. These doors are not of the instructional realm. They are the doors needed for teachers to *engage themselves* differently.

Solution Summary

- Today's learners are begging for more autonomy through *learning by doing*.

- With teaching and learning becoming enmeshed in the social networking frenzy, there is a structural problem that exists if teachers and administrators do not feel a fundamental sense of urgency to change how students will learn in their classrooms.
- Moving forward, children will beg for exhibitions of instructional mastery through the use of technology, of which they will most likely know more about than the adults in the building.
- Monitor your own social networking accessibility and usage so that you are not putting yourself in an undermining position of authority through the use of visuals posted, thoughts and feelings exposed, or other notable items that may cause professional conflicts.

In this chapter, there was an abundance of caution leveled at the use of technology as an educator. Because of the online tools students have at their disposal, how students learn and relate to one another has obviously changed from many years past. Gatekeeping these changes is quite the challenge for teachers, administrators, and parents. In turn, these changes should also serve as a personal reminder, for those who work with children every day, that your online profile and actions are accessible and processed by others. The impact this can have on the perception of your professional disposition may inhibit your ability to carry forward some of the messaging you would like to create for students and parents.

Remember, being aware of your online actions, as a professional, is part of being professional. To protect yourself and the perceptions others have of you (because perception is reality), it behooves all educators to raise their awareness levels about personal postings and online interactions.

Chapter Fifteen

Is Teaching the Profession for You?

Questioning if you are in the right profession is common for anybody working in any organization. Almost everyone asks themselves these questions throughout their working life. It is no different in the schools. This chapter will focus on how one teacher reframed her disposition around the profession with the support of her administrator, essentially flipping her mindset upside down.

CASE STUDY: JESSICA

After working in the profession for four years and earning high marks, Jessica, a third-grade teacher, came to her assistant principal and stated in late May, "I've recently come to the conclusion that this job is unfair. I get blamed often. The e-mails I receive from parents demean my professional construct. I am so demoralized." Jessica had taught at the elementary level all of her beginning years and initially enjoyed everything about the profession. It was her true passion.

She knew that the teaching profession had dramatically changed since her mom retired after thirty years in the classroom. She knew the expectations and accountability measures had met unprecedented technology-laced highs. Nevertheless, progress reports, grading, assessment practices, and statewide expectations did not prevent her from enjoying what she loved: teaching children. However, the more she focused on the future, the more her decision to stay in the profession long term was filled with anxiety and fear. "Could I do this for twenty-six more years? Do I deserve to be treated this way?" she pondered.

On a warm and humid afternoon in May, Jessica conjured up the courage to come into the office and talk to the person that hired her. She shared exactly why she was scared. The perspectives she described were real. Once she was done, Jessica had envisioned that her administrator would drum up a rebuttal that would change her way of thinking. Having known him for many years, she could predict his response. The administrative team did not want her to leave. They knew she was one of their strongest instructors at this grade level. Then, in a few short words, the assistant principal shocked Jessica with his response. He stated, "Jessica, teaching just may not be for you."

He likened his perspective to a book titled *Marriage Isn't for You*. In the book, author Seth Adam Smith discusses a theme around the phrase "marriage is not for you." It is about the person you marry. Through his own insight and experiences, Seth realized what commitment, dedication, and loving the other is all about under the umbrella term of *marriage*. In this example, much like in the book *Marriage Isn't for You*, the assistant principal patterned his thoughts, through this marriage lens set forth by Smith, by speaking about how to make relationships stronger by reviewing how you view your relationship with children. "You don't teach to discover a sense of happiness for yourself," he uttered.

You teach to educate another mind other than your own. In the classroom, you operate in a world that wants you to believe that you pursue your dream, train for it, prepare for it, and once you land *that job*, it will solve your dreams. When it doesn't, it is because your expectations of what teaching is supposed to provide you may be skewed. Teaching isn't providing you what you had expected because, presently, you may not be accepting a larger picture.

As Jessica heard this perspective, she became frustrated but wanted to listen. "The profession is about teaching others; it's about *their* families, *their* challenges, and *their* expectations of you as their child's instructor. Teaching is about them," he said as he pointed to the yearbook. "In order to see this, you need to develop a tougher outer shell about the comments from parents. Taking offense to the comments of parents is natural, but it also highlights your weakness. You are letting the words of others dramatically impact your state of mind. You are giving them too much power because you are allowing those words and those e-mails to eat away at your mood. It is affecting you at home and it wants to drive you away from what you love most. It is like going through therapy. Until you live through the most difficult sessions, you will not truly understand what I am saying; yet until you adopt this attitude, teaching just may not be in your future long term."

It was in that very moment where the assistant principal gambled. By telling Jessica this, he thought she would immediately vacate the premises. She did. The next morning Jessica came to see the administrator. "I realized that you were absolutely right," Jessica stated.

I want to be happy because of what I do every day. Until our talk yesterday, I didn't think that was an unreasonable expectation. Watching my mother all those years come home and grade papers, I thought I knew what this was all about and I came to you in hopes of getting some direction. However, what you stated goes against all conventional wisdom I have held about myself and teaching. I was angry yesterday afternoon.

I was up all night reflecting on your statement that teaching may not be in my future. I guess I never pondered, at a deeper level, the true meaning of a selfless profession. I had always refrained from using this term *selfless profession* because it smacked a feel of negativity about what I do every day. I thought it was a depressing term. However, your comments redefined my outlook on selfless. Teaching is never about me. It is about the kids in front of me today. It is about serving their needs.

For the first four years of my career, I have harbored some resentment about various decisions and comments from others and allowed those episodes to make me more cynical and defensive. But instead of reminding myself of the faces I adore each day and why I am here, I allowed the bitterness to stimulate strong thoughts about a career change.

Jessica stated that it would take time for her to live these theories emotionally. She said, "I hope to get to a point in my career where I can believe this: you either live every day and truly understand what teaching means, or you will never get it. You will always be resentful toward the profession and allow that pain to manifest itself through complaining to the administration and seeking justice."

"Emotionally exhausted teachers are at risk of becoming cynical and callous and may eventually feel they have little to offer or gain from continuing, and so drop out of the teaching workforce" (Jennings and Greenberg 2009). At the surface, the relationship between emotional exhaustion and individuals leaving the profession seems to be understandable. However, if you peel back this term *emotional exhaustion*, it becomes clear that your mindsets drive your feelings. If you work toward accepting that many of the challenges that exist are not in your control, then emotional exhaustion will not symbolize your daily experiences. Remember, many times, finding success habits that are constructive can be accomplished by looking at others as a role model.

Jo-Ellan Dimitrius discusses in her book *Reading People* how to understand and predict the behaviors of others anytime and anyplace. Her book discusses how to recognize verbal and nonverbal cues to assist us in predicting behavior. Understanding these signals can teach you how these individuals nurture a positive mindset in the chaos of any given day. As Dimitrius discusses, "Unless you learn to hear, really hear, a person's replies, all your questioning may be a complete waste of time." Thus, take time to listen to the people who have served in the profession for many more years. They can teach you how to navigate your feelings in more productive ways.

Many individuals with a compressed mindset, such as Jessica's, dwell on e-mails and interactions for many days. Why was the student not disciplined further? Why is this parent attacking me? Why am I the one who must plan everything? Why am I "looping" again this year? This "why me" role can be very destructive to your internal state of mind. Simply put, you forget to teach yourself coping skills and the importance of solution-oriented dispositions.

As Mihaly Csikszentmihalyi discussed in his book *Flow: The Psychology of Optimal Experience*, happiness is not something that happens. It is a condition that must be cultivated and defended by each person. Those who learn to control inner experiences will be able to determine the quality of their lives. As you relate this back to your classroom experience and other duties as assigned, it is important to recognize this philosophy as a guiding principle. Use your "why me" moments as reminders that you are the only one who can control the quality of your experiences.

Solution Summary

- Verbal and nonverbal cues assist us in predicting behavior.
- Finding success habits that are constructive can be accomplished by simply observing others as role models.
- Taking offense to some of the comments of parents, a colleague, a student, or a friend is natural, but, if not forgotten, they can serve as a ruminating weakness for you.
- Happiness is not something that happens. It is a condition that must be cultivated and defended by each person.

In this chapter, you find some nuggets about how to read other people and make more sense of your surroundings. Actions speak louder than words, but oftentimes so do nonverbal signals in and around the school. Understanding the hidden messages that some colleagues or some parents are sending you is critical to increasing your percentage chance of responding to these individuals in a manner that appeases them without giving in to your own desires on the job.

This cultivating happiness theory can seem obtuse, at first, if you are not accustomed to seeing your moods as negotiable equations that you can control. Defending your sense of happiness is more about (a) watching how your own thoughts, habitually, respond to the stressor and (b) creating space from the noun that is causing you to become irritated. Notice that both of these ideas about defending your happiness are not asking you to blame an outside entity or put responsibility onto someone else. Again, from the reading, you know that they may very well be the reason for your unhappiness; at that moment, however, it is only carried forward by your inability to stop ruminating about it to yourself and with colleagues in the building.

Chapter Sixteen

Resiliency

Don't Let You Beat You and the Roles We Play at School

The "Don't Let You Beat You" philosophy is based on the premise that the person you are with the most in life—the one you spend the most time with—is yourself. It will always be your number one job, your number one responsibility, to make that person proud. Other people's opinions are important, but they should not author your emotions. This chapter will discuss how you can continue to build that mental resiliency muscle by analytically looking at the roles you and your colleagues may play in the school.

Not beating yourself means following your passion, following your heart, and doing the things that you are excited about pursuing in education. For example, once you graduate from "something," emotions such as happiness and joy are at the forefront of your mind. But the true reason behind all of that happiness—the true reason why you are satisfied—is because you earned something. The key to changing how you approach your daily routines, in the classroom or the school, is to recognize how and when you might be beating yourself.

In their book *Mindful Teacher*, Dennis Shirley and Elizabeth MacDonald cite an analysis on how school policy reforms can become tainted by problems of implementation and build a sense of cynicism among teachers: "Because the rise of professional learning communities occurred concurrently with the rise of the accountability movement, the openness that appeared to be promised through genuine teacher collaboration easily became captive to the drive to study and then increase pupil test scores. What you can learn from the concurrent movements is that one initiative can overpower another quite quickly" (Shirley and MacDonald 2009).

The term *abstract progression* is a way to remind yourself to look for a sense of different or not the norm with relation to your decision making. There are thousands of verbal and nonverbal messages that outline your experiences from one school week to the next. From everyday conversations, e-mails, text messages, social networking sites, the Internet, and so on, you are influenced. If not recognized and cultivated appropriately, you can lose the ability to recognize when and how to make the best decisions for yourself. For example, one e-mail you receive, after second block, can send you on a downward slide. You may interpret the content (first leg of the triangle) and attach meaning to it (second leg), and then your emotions follow. You can feel the anxiety build internally because of the event that is happening externally.

You know there is no quick fix, yet we seemingly often beg to find one. If the self-checkout line at the grocery store is broken, you might find thoughts that resemble the following: *this place never has its act together*. If the person in front of you at the checkout line is using coupons and causing you to wait for a much longer time than you had anticipated, you may find yourself becoming frustrated with that individual. Yet, as you review this type of rationale, it makes no sense.

By getting frustrated with the individual in front of you, who is simply using coupons to save money, you are illuminating your lack of knowledge or skill set to recognize that this person is not the problem. It is the situation. The reality is the fact that you are frustrated with the happenchance surrounding your situation and displacing it onto a perfectly innocent individual. Using such mundane day-to-day experiences allows you to practice and strengthen the muscle/habit called resiliency.

HOW DO YOU STRENGTHEN THIS RESILIENCY MUSCLE IN THE MOMENT?

You don't. As you have learned from this book, feelings and emotions are naturally going to arise and you should not seek to stop that relationship because it is a concretized dyad. Strengthening your resiliency is not about stopping yourself from becoming frustrated; you can't just turn that emotion off. This is not what the self-assessment you took or the postulates of this book are asking you to do.

What you can do is learn how to channel these feelings, *while they are happening*, and remind yourself of the fixation habit that causes you to ruminate about past experiences and blame others. Part of improving your resiliency is to observe your frustrating emotions *internally* while the incident is occurring—recognize the feeling you have when you are reading the offensive e-mail, forwarding it to friends or colleagues, posting your opinions, and so on. These actions feel good because initially you are channeling your frustrated state elsewhere. However, this forwarding and reacting/posting syndrome creates a deeper wedge with your emotional construct.

Your feelings become validated by friends (or strangers), and you automatically become even more influenced and angrier with others. Your attitudes, emotional states, and behaviors essentially become, in a sense, hijacked. Your mindset is now a product of what others are creating for you, with their own written words, responses, and posted opinions. Logical assumptions need cognitive empathy.

What does that mean?

Assumptions are the product of habitual thoughts based on experiences. You cannot assume anything without having experienced a similar moment in the past. How does this relate to your life in the schools? You understand that assumptions are dangerous in the classroom when you are looking at individual students. For administrators, this concept would be when you are looking at teachers. You understand the importance of maintaining an opened mindset for everyone involved. However, adults can also be very quick with the assumption tool, especially about themselves or their own children.

CASE STUDY: IT'S AUGUST!

While working with a group of teachers at a summer retreat in August, the administrative team asked the instructors to create a list of stressful assumptions they possessed regarding the school year. The goal was to have the teachers identify the annual, recurring triggers that caused stress. They mapped out these *trigger times* from the first quarter through June. They identified, by referencing the calendar, all of the events or experiences that symbolized those sticky situations throughout a given school year that caused stress.

Most importantly, for the administrative team, they wanted to uncover the frames of reference the teachers were using to view the upcoming school year. As background, this teaching team had many personality conflicts and had relationship challenges each year. To better understand the team dynamics of this case, it helped to take a more clinical approach to its existence. By dissecting the personality traits of these individuals, the administrators were able to gain a deeper understanding about the reasons behind their choices. The administrators believed that by learning more about *the why* behind the colleagues you disagree with, you can at least become more desensitized toward their behaviors (albeit, admittedly, this is very difficult).

By adopting a family systems perspective to this group of teachers, the administrators were able to support the individual needs of the teachers more efficiently. The teachers on this team, like others, live with each other every day. They confide in one another about their personal and professional lives throughout a given school year. At times, they support one another when they are not feeling their best. However, the personalities on this team were very strong and clashed throughout the years.

Team meetings often have defined roles with norms for behavior (much like family systems). Because each team has a leader, it is helpful to consider and define what roles each colleague adopts, for example, within a professional learning community. The most experienced teacher may take on the parental role, which, at times, depending on the other family members, can be perceived as condescending to the teammates. Resentment, on the seasoned teacher's part, may build as she is constantly having to share and review her practices with others—and not receiving the gratitude that she expected. This was true in this case study. Dysfunctional families (or in this case the instructional team) divide up the emotional responsibilities via specific roles.

From a family systems perspective, the family hero, in this particular team's makeup, was the science teacher who was the leader of the group. She was admired and seemed to have it all together. She was very responsible and made the team look very good to the outsiders. She was often perceived as quiet, but when the doors closed and ten months transpired, the parents were raving about her and requesting their next child be in her classroom. The family hero was admired by others on the team, except by the injustice collector (to be discussed later).

The scapegoat was the math teacher who often felt misunderstood. She seemed to harbor a lot of blame and bad publicity from parents and felt very insecure, like a victim in her own classroom. The administration was always needing to talk to her more than anybody. Though she would never attest to her belief publicly, this teacher confided to the administration that she felt rejected by her colleagues and the parents.

The lost child teacher was the very quiet one. This was the history teacher. She stayed out of the fray and could not wait to shut the classroom door and do what she wanted. From the outsider's perspective, she seemed quiet, creative, and avoidant of conflict. During team meetings, the lost child tried not to be noticed at all. She would not contribute to much of the discussion and needed to be encouraged to take risks with her colleagues.

The mascot, the teaching assistant, was the one who used humor to break the tension. The mascot teacher sensed the tension that the injustice collector was creating. She often tried to break the stress with a joke or a quick change in topic.

In his book *Healing from Family Rifts*, Mark Sichel discusses the term *the injustice collector*. The true problem in group dynamics, such as the teaching team described above, is when one teacher is an injustice collector. The "injustice collecting" teacher, in this case, was the English instructor. This was the role that caused the most stress within the team. Injustice collectors believe they are never wrong because they are always right. They very rarely apologize for their actions and, essentially, they feel morally superior because they have taught longer. These individuals will quickly dismiss ideas for the group and speak for the group to the administration—even if they are not dubbed the team leader.

Injustice collectors will undermine the efforts of the family members (other teachers) by sending e-mails to them (colleagues) and CCing the principal. Injustice collectors oftentimes will choose e-mail to communicate issues to their colleagues. They may refute the creative ideas of others by stating: "I already tried that years ago and it didn't work." It's yet another, maybe even subconscious, control strategy for them to tell the rest of the family that they know more. They have the answers of what to do and how to do it. A clear sign that you may be dealing with an injustice collector is when you offer a rebuttal to them. In fact, there may be times where the injustice collector subconsciously seeks another's opinion in order to have perspectives to refute. Expressing a different opinion, at that point, probably is not changing anything. Habitually, the collector rationalizes that the fault lies with others and truly believes this.

As opposed to focusing on the dangers of perceptions, predictions, and judgments onto others, the injustice collector will make the issue a right or wrong (fair or unfair) concept. There is an overwhelming desire to be right or to convince others they are wrong. However, this is short-lived when they are not confronted with a disagreeing entity.

In other words, as the moment is happening, if people cease to be argumentative or disagreeable or state their opinion, the injustice collectors have no conflict. They are forced to reflect on their own behaviors and reactions. Because these individuals have hung their sense of self on the need to be right by keeping everyone else at fault for their own personal dysfunction, the injustice collectors rarely take accountability. They lack the ability to show introspection and contrition. These may be the individuals who wield a judgmental wand after every family event, workplace decision, friendship interaction/posting. The people around them feel like they are truly walking on eggshells; the injustice collector is like a porcupine and you don't know how to approach them. Everyone else has done a disservice to them. They feel they are doing the most. They are the victim when it is convenient.

In order to feel justified in their opinions, this personality type will throw itself into justification mode with others who will listen. The phone will be picked up or the text/post will be sent to describe the situation to multiple parties. It is through this type of complaining to others that the injustice collectors feel justified and proven right; yet they will endlessly claim that this is not the reason for their action. In fact, when confronted with this rationalization about their motives, the injustice collectors can almost become maniacal in their efforts to deny and suppress the truth. The final outcome to this emotional cycle of dysfunction tends to be an unhappy or unfulfilled individual who possesses a small sense of who they really are.

To help in their justification, injustice collectors may bring additional personnel into the equation: "Others think like me. They see it too. It isn't just me. See, these innocent, third-party entities agree with me. I have the right approach and it is the other (person, place, or thing/idea) that is wrong." The insecurities in these justifications are ramped. Their sense of self is simply a house of cards waiting to be knocked down, almost daily, so it can locate conflict, claim that something else is at fault, and then wallow in self-imposed suffering when it doesn't *go their way*.

In this particular team, these roles were clearly symbolic of how these four teachers functioned. They dreaded meeting with one another predominately because of the injustice collector. In August, already, the other three teachers felt like the injustice collector would find any topic or problem discussed as the fault of others. It will be the administration's lack of _____ or another teacher's perceived unwillingness to _____ or a parent who doesn't do _____. If the librarian would just do _____ or if the counselor would do more of _____, then things would be better.

After many years of the injustice collector disagreeing with colleagues at work, in this case study, the administrators confronted her on how to improve her situation at this retreat. They talked to her about how to find refuge, ironically, in relinquishing the desire to express an opinion on everything. The suppression of opinion is difficult for the injustice collector. Without engagement, conflict is minimized and the injustice collectors have nothing to collect. By relinquishing this desire of expression at all costs, they can begin to liberate themselves from that emotional chain binding myth: always stick up for what you believe in. It seems rather absurd to refer to suppression as a healthy component to anything. However, with injustice collectors, it can stimulate the change they need to get back to respecting the culture of their personal and professional relationships.

It is never wise to paint with a broad brush and group the personality types of any organization into one category, thus one must focus on the individual. As the administrators worked with this particular teacher, unfortunately, it was apparent that she was not going to change. After many meetings, the administrators met with the team to conduct an exercise. Before they started, the administrative team stressed the following: if someone disagrees with a request or suggestion in the team meetings throughout the year, just say no. They wanted to give the other teachers a green light to say no (to the injustice collector), but it was stated more broadly. Trying to please certain individuals is never going to be possible, thus, speak up for yourself and say no to them. It is a simple answer to a very complex issue.

In order for the teachers' motivation to grow, the administrators asked the teachers to write down their assumptions about the year and record the specific experiences they wanted to avoid. For example, some items were listed as follows:

- a lot of meetings
- too many students in my class
- contentious parent conferences
- committee obligations
- colleagues not pulling their own weight
- colleague tension and people wanting things their way

The teachers knew that these were nonnegotiable facets of the job, but they assumed these were the causes to their stress. Kegan and Lahey discuss in their book *Immunity to Change* about how to recognize and cultivate the individual's motivation to grow. They utilize the analogy of an immunity X-ray map to discuss how improvement goals are thwarted by our own obstructive behaviors such as lack of directness, overconsulting, and constant efforts to please (Kegan and Lahey 2009). Their discussion on change prevention systems is a constructive perspective on how you can establish subconscious habits and hidden commitments that prevent you from reaching certain emotional states.

In this professional development exercise for teachers, the administrative team wanted the instructors to view their self-generated list of stressors as symbolic to their previous experiences. This was a logical assumption. Now, the goal was for the administrative team to take these logical assumptions and validate the teacher's concerns. They also explained that the items the teachers listed will continue to be experiences on the job. However, this exercise allowed them to see how their reactionary state could be altered. Writing down the stressors, discussing their feelings about them, and then connecting with one another on how to influence their mindsets for the better was the task.

Whether it is dubbed the immunity muscle or resiliency, confronting these negative habits, accordingly, in August, for the classroom teacher, allowed an empathetic tone to exist. There were not any deadlines as of yet and the school year had not begun. Thus, the willingness to try something new was ripe in August. In this forum, the administrators acknowledged the teachers' assumptions in a manner that justified and supported their needs. Specifically, the principal spoke to some choices or action steps the teachers could take to improve how they reacted to the list of stressors that they generated:

1. Analyze how you have reacted to these previous experiences in the past.
2. Adopt a philosophy that views these items as educational givens. Accept no control over the outcomes.
3. Hold yourself more accountable for when your mood is shifted by any one of these stressors you listed. In other words, for this school year, this self-generated list of stressors will serve as the accountable checklist for what you were *not* going to be able to use as excuse for your frustration. The checklist was a visual reminder for the teachers to work toward not letting these specific outside circumstances/decisions impact their quality of life on the job or at home.

The principal, essentially, wanted the teachers to journal in August about the most stressful situations that occur throughout a given school year. He then wanted to use that list, almost like a contract, where the teachers would agree to try very hard not to fixate or complain about the items on the list. This forced the teachers to, emotionally and mentally, build a stronger sense of resiliency.

Over the course of the year, the teachers reported that they found a stronger rhythm to their day. Because they were holding themselves more accountable about not stressing around the items recorded in August, it allowed a more positive foundation to build around their mindsets for each quarter. Their family systems roles stayed the same, but the exercise itself coupled with just saying no to the injustice collector diffused stress and created a more positive culture within the dynamics of the team.

Solution Summary

- The key to changing how you approach your daily routines, in the classroom or the school, is to recognize how and when you might be beating yourself.
- Abstract progression is a way to remind yourself to look for a sense of different or not the norm with relation to your decision making.
- The reality is the fact that you are frustrated with the happenchance surrounding your situation and displacing it onto a perfectly innocent individual. Using such mundane day-to-day experiences allows you to practice and strengthen the muscle/habit called resiliency.
- Learn how to channel your perceptions of experiences, *while they are happening*, and remind yourself of the fixation habit that can cause you to ruminate about past experiences and blame others.
- Assumptions are the product of habitual thoughts based on experiences. You cannot assume anything without having experienced a similar moment in the past.

Aside from reviewing your assumptions and typical response mechanisms to situations, this chapter speaks a great deal about family roles being symbolic of how some teaching teams may operate in schools. The personality types, in any group dynamics, can be challenging. If you can adopt a greater under-standing of how, subconsciously, these roles play themselves out throughout a given school year, you can begin to build a more resilient mindset toward the challenges that some personalities may present. Discovering how others define perceived injustices on the job and how often they perseverate on them is a very important observational note for you to carry forward. This recognition serves as a reminder to your internal compass of emotions to not let others try to bring you into their lane of complaining and blaming.

Chapter Seventeen

Backward Design and Winning Differently

In this final chapter, you will learn how to use a very common educational term to see how you can apply it to personal growth. In addition, the term *pride* will be discussed in great detail. As discussed, prior to beginning any type of self-improvement regimen, your ability to look at yourself is the first step. Taking pride in what you do each and every day should be part of that self-improvement checklist as well.

The backbone of any successful educational framework and lesson design should always begin with the end in mind. The backward design philosophy can be applied to the mental constructs for reframing your mindset as well. Professionally, you ask what you want your students to know, how you know they know it, and what you are going to do if they don't. Personally, it might look like this: *How do I want to feel, how am I going to know I am feeling this, and what am I going to do if I don't?* In a lesson for students, you construct steps to make students successful and provide them opportunities to display how their efforts have met an objective. Then you construct assessments that measure that progress to discover how you know they know it and take further action if they don't.

In life, outside of the classroom, one should take a similar path. You need to construct your own development plan, one that will create a platform that embraces challenges in a constructive way. Some people are very good at reframing their attitudes toward perceived injustices. Others need tools to flip their mindset for a better way of living. Then, as a leader for yourself, your classrooms, and the school, you need to construct self-assessment *check-ins* to measure that progress and discover *how you know* you are improving. And then, if you are not achieving these states, hopefully you will possess the tools for taking further action to reframe an attitude for the better.

143

Maintaining flexibility with your assumptions is not an easy task but an important step to this reframing process. To truly be authentic when dissecting your assumptions, you should conduct an autopsy of your actions and decisions from the past. Oftentimes, you may want to think and believe that your decisions about students, colleagues, family members, and yourself have been accurate or, at the very least, acceptable courses of action. Pride can sometimes be an overlooked personal characteristic because, at times, this term can be viewed as egocentric. Yet, that is not what this word means. When reviewing this word more closely, you can take a cue from a principal who used the word *pride* with his opening remarks to the staff in August. He broke down the word pride as the following:

P stands for Perseverance. Many teachers and administrators feel, at the beginning of their careers, proud of their accomplishments and even more proud of their first classroom or first management job. Perseverance is the body of work you have put into the walls of the school. There was a time in your life where you couldn't wait to talk about the progress of your students or the great new teachers you hired. Don't ever lose that sense of pride. You don't get to lead the lives of children and teachers for ten months out of a given year without having learned what it means to work hard, to fail, and to bounce back. When your students don't do well on a test and you spiral back your instruction and they improve, that's perseverance. The results they achieve, however, do not serve as a symbol of perseverance. The hours of time you spent on reteaching a student or working with a struggling teacher and trying new ways of reaching them—that's perseverance. Getting home, getting dinner ready for the family, and sitting down at 9:00 at night to formulate a lesson plan or write up an evaluation on a teacher—that's perseverance.

R stands for Reflective. You cannot be successful unless you have the ability to reflect on making decisions that are best for you. This is a powerful skill that will erode if you are not careful. Reflecting on yourself allows you to stay focused on your goals. Some of those reflections are going to be more difficult than others. Constant reflection allows for constant learning. And then before you know it, you acquire one of the most important traits in life: wisdom. Wisdom is not something that is given to you. Wisdom is something you earn. Perseverance and reflection are married to one another. Part of you being a highly motivated and self-actualized teacher or school-based administrator is your ability to *reflect on how you have succeeded.*

I team. The "I" in pride is looking back at you in the mirror as you get ready for school every morning. "I" should be celebrated more often. Give yourself permission to focus on "I." You see, so often as you get older, that "I" is baked into a team or some organization where multiple individuals must work together for the common good. Define your success team. Your family of origin, your spouse, your friends, your colleagues—any one of them can be part of your success team.

As you start a new school year, who will be on your success team? Who are you going to surround yourself with to be successful? Before you hit send, before you walk into that school, before you choose the committees you will serve on, you must ask yourself two simple questions: *How will I engage myself differently this year? How will I win differently?* That is ultimately what will guide you to grow more and experience more success.

D stands for Develop. Understanding the process of developing and being patient with how to succeed is the key. Never stop developing. You have control over how you are going to develop yourself from this day forward. Developing is a lifelong process. It's not a skill. It's not something you and your success team can mold because life is too unpredictable. But what you can do is prepare. Developing into a better person each and every day means acknowledging your mistakes and overcoming them. There are people in your life who may never have to work as hard as you to get there. Fifty percent of the people in this world are going to be more skilled than you and 50 percent will not be as skilled. Deal with that notion and work your way out of the middle.

E stands for Engaged. Engage people around you. In order to be successful, you have to be willing to engage, build relationships, and ask questions. If you want opportunities and you want to minimize your frustration levels, seek to learn more by developing further as a person, before trying to improve your professional construct. As long as you stay engaged, life will give you opportunities. The people who don't get it, the people who are always struggling, they are the ones who refuse to change who they are because of one inhibiting belief: *This is what I have always done and it is who I am.* If you can engage yourself by befriending the right people at the right time in life, you will be successful. The choice and the responsibility is in your hands.

Life is not a scoreboard. If you want to win, you need to win with yourself. Pride is about winning differently with yourself. Winning differently, by way of acquiring a refocused, task-driven mind in the classroom, begins with understanding how you think throughout any given day. It's about knowing how to navigate your emotional state differently than how you have done it in the past. Pride and *winning with yourself* is all that matters. When you can adopt a different mindset with a focus on reframing your old habits of the mind, you can experience a deeper sense of success both in education and in your personal life.

Solutions Summary

- The backbone of any successful educational framework and lesson design should always begin with the end in mind.
- Professionally, you ask what you want your students to know, how you know they know it, and what you are going to do if they don't. Personally, it might look like this: how do I want to feel, how am I going to know I am feeling this, and what am I going to do if I don't?
- You need to construct self-assessments *check-ins* to measure that progress and discover *how you know* you are improving.
- As long as you stay engaged, life will give you opportunities.
- Life is not a scoreboard. If you want to win, you need to win with yourself. Pride is about winning differently with yourself.

In this last chapter, you learned about the engine that keeps your willingness to change consistent for long periods of time. In other words, the more you can develop a strong sense of pride about what you do each day for students and their families, the more you will build a resilience to the challenges of the classroom and the school. Learning to stay engaged means that you want to create opportunities for yourself.

 If you want to think differently, act differently, and just live differently in your mind each and every day, it starts with staying engaged with a desire to change your mindset. It starts with admitting and accepting that you want to improve personally, which in turn will impact you professionally. Staying in the comforts of your conceptual prisms about *your lot in life* or how *these were the cards you were dealt* will only exacerbate a fixed mindset that works against you. Working your way out of a negative mindset starts with diagramming mentally how to change your thoughts. With a strong dedication to trying something different, building these mental triangles analytically will create habits of the mind that serve as catalysts for positive change in both your personal and professional lives.

Appendix A: Playbook of Professional Development Exercises for School Staff

Five Plays Teachers and Administrators Can Run, as a Staff, to Win over Their Mindsets

Learning Key

Understanding the concepts within the book is not enough. Retention rates drive the effectiveness of professional development. It is not the speaker, the author, the content, or the "take-aways" that make a difference. There have been many professional development symposiums that you have been exposed to in your career. How many of them have not stuck? Many individuals are motivated to return to their schools and share the information—train the trainer methods for staff development. As is the case with any organization, because of a variety of influential factors, some members of the school get it and apply it. Others just cannot board the energy bus to try something different.

This playbook is not about convincing the others. In fact, it is not about convincing anybody. It is simply an awareness tool to help you get started in reframing your mindset by way of catching your thoughts via mental diagramming. Before we get to the learning outcomes and how teachers and administrators can conduct professional development around these concepts, please review the diagram below.

Accepting that you want to change and buying into new concepts that ask you to challenge your belief systems requires one prerequisite: holding steadfast to the Learning Pyramid. You must be willing to get yourself (and the staff) to the participatory teaching methods of the triangle consistently. Re-

The Learning Pyramid*

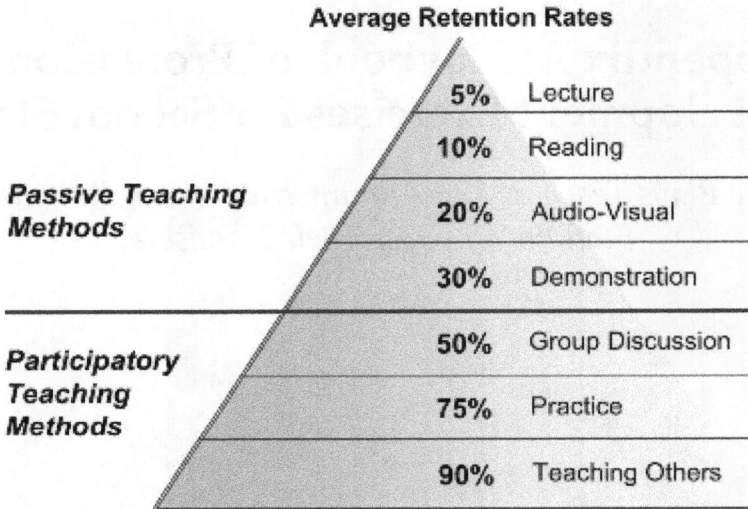

Average Retention Rates

	5%	Lecture
	10%	Reading
Passive Teaching Methods	20%	Audio-Visual
	30%	Demonstration
	50%	Group Discussion
Participatory Teaching Methods	75%	Practice
	90%	Teaching Others

*Adapted from National Training Laboratories, Washington, D.C.

The Learning Pyramid. Adapted from National Training Laboratories, Washington, D.C.

member, a lot of what closing your personal achievement gap is about is simply teaching yourself how to recognize your thoughts, accept the feelings around them, and then work toward not ruminating. In order to accomplish this task consistently and reframe your mindset for the better, group discussions, practice, and teaching others are the key. The habits of the mind are then created and you can begin to adopt a new system of beliefs and reactions around the experiences that once caused you stress, anxiety, and confusion.

Outcomes

By taking the ME-SA, processing the results, and applying their findings to the triangle methods for reframing their mindset, participants will be able to:

1. Define their most common triggers for stress and anxiety.
2. Define their habitual reactions to these triggers.

3. Discuss the reasons behind these habits of the mind—where the blame goes.
4. Diagram these triggers and reactions in the triangles.
5. Discuss the findings with partners.
6. Explore ways to contract with themselves on what will not serve as excuses or blaming entities moving forward.
7. Plan for next steps in creating a culture for the school that focuses on the Learning Pyramid's participatory teaching methods—Getting Involved and Not Taking Sides.

TWO CIRCLES EXERCISE

Objective: To learn more from others about their experience with the ME-SA and what their results mean to them.

Action Item:

- Read the descriptions and results of your ME-SA.
- Go back to the questions that you were *on the fence about* in regard to your answer and mark those down.
- Break into two large groups based on whether you are in Group A or Group B.
- Discuss the assessment and your feelings about the process. Everyone needs to participate in this discussion. Using a talking stick or a ball to act as the microphone can help. (*) Specifically, speak to those you were on the fence about and why.
- Once completed, half of the people in each circle will then switch to the other circle with which they were not part of before.
- In these circles, the new participants should share out what was discussed in their previous circle.
- This process should be repeated for the other two halves.
- Return back to your original circles and, as a group, pick the top five questions (from the ME-SA or from your discussions) that you found to be most fruitful for further analysis.

Last Step: At this stage, it is time to fill out three charts with sticky dots. Each individual will post dots on the first two charts and one person, who represents the original circle, will fill out Chart #3. Finally, discuss the postings and learn from one another.

AGREE   DISAGREE   Top 5

I agreed with most of the results from this assessment.	I disagreed with most of the results from this assessment.	The following 5 numbers represent the questions our circle found to be most intriguing to discuss:

THE SUCCESS DIAGRAMMING EXERCISE

For this exercise, each individual will fill out triangles to better learn how to diagram their triggers and their emotional responses/feelings about those stimulants when they occur. The third leg (the dotted) will stay open for the initial part of the exercise.

There will be seven SUCCES(*)S triangles to dissect (S: School, U: Urgent, C: Curriculum, C: Communication, E: E-mail, S: Students, and S: Social). For each one, participants should record the top five stressors as they pertain to the triangle descriptions *and* the three most dominating feelings/emotions about them (sad, angry, frustrated, jealous).

- *The School Triangle:* This is a triangle about what stresses you the most about your job in education.
- *The Urgent Triangle:* This is a personal triangle. For this symbol, participants should record the five most pressing (urgent) "things" that are happening in their life right now. It can be very personal (family issues, finances, relationships, car troubles, etc.). Then record the first three most dominating feelings or reactions to them.
- *The Curriculum Triangle:* This is a triangle about what stresses you the most about your curriculum this year. It may be a new curriculum guide, mapping, linking standards with assessments, and so on.
- *The Communication Triangle:* This is a triangle about what stresses you the most about communicating with colleagues, parents, administration, and students. This is the triangle where you might record a phrase "trouble with colleague" or "parent conferences" or "meetings in general" or "I

have to present" or "be the team lead." All of these are communication roles.

- *E-mail:* For this triangle, what are the stressors that manifest themselves throughout the entire school year as they relate to e-mail (parents e-mailing, being CC'd on an e-mail, blind copied, principal's e-mail, countywide mandate e-mails for new training requirements, always having to respond to e-mails when there is no time, reply-all e-mails, etc.)? Again, phrases may be needed for this triangle.
- *Students:* For the student triangle, what are the stressors that come about with children most consistently?
- (*) *Social:* This is another personal triangle. For this symbol, participants should view this last triangle as an opportunity to list the five *experiences* they wish they had more of in their life or that they wish were better. This has nothing to do with school. Examples: relationships, exercising, pursuing interests, etc. Participants should be sure to list their current emotional reactions/feelings to not having that right now.
- *STOP: DO NOT READ ANY FURTHER UNTIL YOU HAVE COMPLETED THE FOLLOWING TRIANGLES.*

School Triangle	Urgent Triangle
1. _____ 2. _____ 3. _____ 4. _____ 5. _____ 1. _____ 2. _____ 3. _____	1. _____ 2. _____ 3. _____ 4. _____ 5. _____ 1. _____ 2. _____ 3. _____
Curriculum Triangle	Communication Triangle
1. _____ 2. _____ 3. _____ 4. _____ 5. _____ 1. _____ 2. _____ 3. _____	1. _____ 2. _____ 3. _____ 4. _____ 5. _____ 1. _____ 2. _____ 3. _____

Email Triangle

1. _____
2. _____
3. _____
4. _____
5. _____

1. _____
2. _____
3. _____

Student Triangle

1. _____
2. _____
3. _____
4. _____
5. _____

1. _____
2. _____
3. _____

Social Triangle

1. _____
2. _____
3. _____
4. _____
5. _____

1. _____
2. _____
3. _____

Building the Resiliency Muscle:

(*) The dotted line of the triangles remains empty. The stressors that the participants recorded in each one of the SUCCESS triangles are very important. Because the participant has chosen these stressors to symbolize why they experience stress and anxiety, he or she must pick a date for when they will begin to take responsibility for that stress. In other words, each participant should write in a date for when he or she is no longer going to ruminate about these issues, talk about them outwardly or allow them to dramatically impact their stress levels.

After completing the triangles, the participants should review their responses to the seven categories and begin a two-fold process. First, they should write down key words or phrases that will influence these challenges for the better (speak directly to the colleague, call the parent, book the social activity, etc.). Secondly, and most importantly, of the challenges listed in each triangle, participants should contract with themselves a specific date for when they will begin to take responsibility for their emotional state about these challenges. At some point, a date needs to be issued by the participant, in order for them to stop blaming the stimulants and start taking action and accountability for their existence.

TAKE 5: I WISH I THOUGHT MORE LIKE THIS AND NOT LIKE THAT

Objective: Participants will learn more about their ME-SA results and from others in terms of looking at their responses through the lens of wishing they were different. For this exercise, participants will work individually to dig deeper into the some of their answers on the ME-SA that they wish were not their answers. In other words, each participant is asked to go back over the questions on the ME-SA and review how they answered them. Of the one hundred questions, each participant should choose five questions where they marked one answer but really wish they thought like the other answer. The question number and the answer they originally chose should be recorded in the space below.

Once recorded, each participant should journal (three to five sentences) about *why they wish they were not like this and more like that*. The goal for this exercise is to get people to not just think along a continuum of where they specifically want to improve but to take action on why this really is bothersome. Again, the five-minute journaling for each question is simply answering the why (why did I mark this and why do I wish I was more like the other response). For this exercise, it is important to stress that participants are not to write about their goals or how to get there or action steps—simply why they wish they were not like this and more like that.

1.
2.
3.
4.
5.

1. Why I wish I was the other one

2. Why I wish I was the other one

3. Why I wish I was the other one

4. Why I wish I was the other one

5. Why I wish I was the other one

After each participant has filled out the above information and provided a description as to why they wish their thoughts or actions resembled the other statement in the question, participants should break into think-pair-share dyads and discuss their journals (learn from others in terms of how they interpreted their answers and what they wish was different about their own personal construct).

ALL FOR ONE AND ONE FOR ALL

Objective: Participants in one school can identify the most common choices found in the ME-SA per question. This will allow for a greater understanding of the staff as a whole and where the preferences of people may exist in reference to problem solving, how people view others, and how they view change.

The *All for One and One for All* method is extremely powerful because it allows for a faculty to view the inner working of people's personalities in a safe and confidential manner. By combining the results as a large group, soft and tentative conclusions could be drawn about a variety of personality topics within the organization. The culture of the staff can become a more informed entity due to the discussion and analysis around the ME-SA from a broader perspective.

Directions: After every participant in the school has completed the ME-SA, the results can be entered into a spreadsheet program and then sorted. Once the data is sorted, participants will be able to view how many people answered A or B for each question. This type of feedback is fun as the staff is able to find some humor in the results; yet nobody's individual results are posted. Facilitators (administrators) can then pinpoint specific questions that *say something* about the staff or how people view change and problem solving in the school.

This exercise can provide an enormous amount of take-aways for teachers and administrators.

MEETING AGENDAS

Objective: The item below is an example of how teachers and administrators could organize their curriculum meetings' or department meetings' agendas. Focusing your agenda to just four to five items and then writing down how the team feels, while solving the problems about those items, is a big step in being more transparent as a team. Transparency breeds a solution-focused mindset because nobody is stewing or ruminating about something. Because feelings have been recorded, progress is more seamless.

Conference Notes

Date: _____

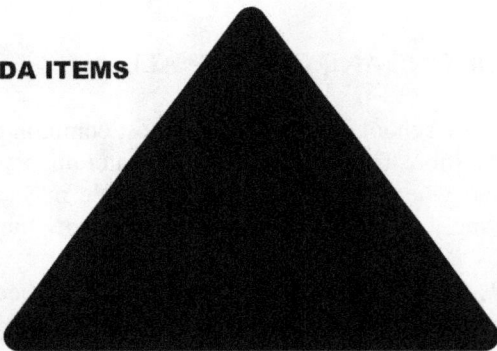

AGENDA ITEMS

1. _____
2. _____
3. _____
4. _____
5. _____

1. _____
2. _____
3. _____

Bibliography

Argyris, Chris. *Teaching Smart People How to Learn*. Boston: Harvard Business Review Classics, 1991.

Bal, Vidula, Michael Campbell, and Sharon Larsen-McDowell. *Managing Leadership Stress*. Greensboro, N.C.: Center for Creative Leadership, 2008.

Brown, Stuart. *Play: How It Shapes the Brain, Opens the Imagination, and Invigorates the Soul*. New York: Penguin Group, 2009.

Burkhauser, Susan. "How Much Do School Principals Matter When It Comes to Teacher Working Conditions?" *Educational Evaluation and Policy Analysis*, March 1, 2017.

Campbell, David. *Leadership Descriptor Participant Workbook*. Hoboken, N.J.: Wiley, 2002.

Conyers, John, and Robert Ewy. *Charting Your Course: Lessons Learned During the Journey Toward Performance Excellence*. Milwaukee: American Society for Quality, 2003.

Couros, George. *The Innovator's Minset: Empower Learning, Unleash Talent, and Lead a Culture of Creativity*. San Diego: Dave Burgess Consulting, 2015.

Csikszentmihalyi, Mihaly. *Flow: The Psychology of Optimal Experience*. New York: Harper Perennial, 1990.

David, Susan. *Emotional Agility: Get Unstuck, Embrace Change, and Thrive in Work and Life*. New York: Avery, 2016.

Deci, Edward, and Richard Ryan. *Self-Determination Theory: Basic Psychological Needs in Motivation, Development, and Wellness*. New York: Guilford Press, 2017.

Dimitrius, Jo-Ellan. *Reading People*. New York: Ballantine Books, 2008.

Dweck, Carol. *Mindset: The New Psychology of Success*. New York: Random House, 2006.

Forward, Susan, and Donna Frazier. *Emotional Blackmail: When the People in Your Life Use Fear, Obligation and Guilt to Manipulate You*. New York: William Morrow Paperbacks, 1998.

Goleman, Daniel. *Emotional Intelligence: Why I Can Matter More Than I.Q.* New York: Bantam Books, 1995.

Gordon, John. *The Energy Bus*. Hoboken, N.J.: Wiley, 2007.

Gross, Sven, Laurenz Jacobshagen, Nicola Kalin, Wolfgang Meier, Norbert Semmer, and Franziska Tschan. "The Effect of Positive Events at Work on After-Work Fatigue: They Matter Most in Face of Adversity." *Journal of Applied Psychology* 96, no. 3 (2011): 654–64.

Haidt, Jonathan. *The Happiness Hypothesis*. New York: Basic Books, 2006.

Heath, Chip, and Dan Heath. *Switch: How to Change Things When Change Is Hard*. New York: Broadway Books, 2010.

Jennings, P. A., and M. Greenberg. "The Prosocial Classroom: Teacher Social and Emotional Competence in Relation to Child and Classroom Outcomes." *Review of Educational Research* 79, no. 1 (2009): 491–525.

Jones, Dewitt. *Everyday Creativity*. Video. TrainingABC, 2013.

Kegan, K., and L. L. Lahey. *Immunity to Change: How to Overcome It and Unlock Potential in Yourself and Your Organization*. Boston: Harvard Business School Publishing, 2009.

Kotter, John P. *Leading Change*. Boston: Harvard Business School Press, 2012.

Lazarus, Richard, and Susan Folkman. *Stress, Appraisal, and Coping*. New York: Springer, 1984.

Mercer, Michael, and Maryann Troiani. *Spontaneous Optimism*. Lake Zurich, Ill.: Castlegate, 1998.

Merzenich, Michael. *Soft-Wired: How the New Science of Brain Plasticity Can Change Your Life*. San Francisco: Parnassus, 2013.

O'Connor, Ken. *A Repair Kit for Grading: 15 Fixes for Broken Grades*. Portland: ETS, 2007.

Patterson, Kerry, Joseph Grenny, Ron McMillan, and Al Switzler. *Crucial Conversations: Tools for Talking When Stakes Are High*. New York: McGraw-Hill, 2002.

Perkins, Betty. *Lion Taming: The Courage to Deal with Difficult People Including Yourself*. Sacramento, Calif.: Tzedakah Publications, 1995.

Pink, Daniel. *Drive*. New York: Riverhead, 2009.

Robbins, Tony. *Awaken the Giant Within*. New York: Simon & Schuster, 1992.

Rodgers, Joann Ellison. "Go Forth in Anger." *Psychology Today*, March 11, 2014.

Shirley, Dennis, and Elizabeth MacDonald. *Mindful Teacher*. New York: Teachers College Press, 2009.

Sichel, Mark. *Healing from Family Rifts*. New York: McGraw-Hill Education, 2004.

Smith, Seth Adam. *Marriage Isn't for You: It's for the One You Love*. Salt Lake City: Shadow Mountain, 2014.

Wagner, Tony. *Creating Innovators: The Making of Young People Who Will Change the World*. New York: Scribner, 2012.

Whitaker, Todd, and Beth Whitaker. *Teaching Matters: Motivating and Inspiring Yourself*. Larchmont, N.Y.: Eye on Education, 2002.

Whitaker, Todd, and Jason Winkle. *Feeling Great: The Educator's Guide for Eating Better, Exercising Smarter and Feeling Your Best*. London: Routledge, 2002.

Wiggins, Grant, and Jay McTighe. *Understanding by Design*. Alexandria, Va.: ASCD, 1998.

Wiggins, Kaye. "Teaching Is Among the Top Three Most Stressed Occupations." tes Institute, June 25, 2015.

Young, Shinzen. "Five Ways to Know Yourself: An Introduction to Basic Mindfulness." Shinzen Young, Unified Mindfulness, June 30, 2016.

Zapf, Dieter. "Emotion Work and Psychological Well-Being: A Review of the Literature and Some Conceptual Considerations." *Human Resource Management Review* 12, no. 2 (2002): 237–68.

About the Author

Todd Elliott Franklin is a principal in the Fairfax County Public School system in Great Falls, Virginia. Todd has served as a school-based administrator at both the elementary and middle school levels. Throughout his career, he has had the fortunate opportunity to work collaboratively with multiple teachers, school administrators, and central office personnel in the field of professional development. Some of those experiences have included leading the math and language arts vertical articulation teams in various schools at the elementary, middle, and high school levels.

Todd has also served, in the central office, as a special projects administrator for the teacher evaluation team in Fairfax County. In this role, he led both personal and online professional development around the instructional and leadership standards for teachers and administrators. His work also included training administrators and central office personnel on how to conduct online observations focused on best practices. As a collaborative team member, with his time in the central office, Todd helped author the language around the performance matrices and goal setting for teachers, administrators, and instructional resource professionals.

Early in his career, Todd served as a guidance counselor and taught peer helping, on the elective cycle, at the middle school level. In this role, he also served as the director of programs for the Northern Virginia Counselor's Association chapter in Fairfax, Virginia. After working in these roles, Todd served as an assistant principal at the middle school level before becoming an elementary school principal. These experiences have provided Todd an opportunity to pursue his passion for working with teachers and administrators in the field of education and mindset strategies that work. He has spent his professional career observing and studying how effective teachers and administrators pursue their love for the profession while adopting a productive mindset that is based on flexibility and focused on solutions.

Todd is married to Maureen, also a former teacher and assistant principal, who served as the middle school language arts specialist for the Fairfax County school system. They are the proud parents of three children: Brendan, Julia, and Ryan.

Todd can be found on Facebook, Twitter (@ToddEFranklin), and via his website, www.toddfranklin.com.